Jackie,
I hope you love reading the book as much as I loved writing it.
-Also - I am so, so, so, sorry that I spelled Payton's name wrong! You know that doesn't mean I don't think she's the

Faking
cutest thing
Normal
ever!

Ramona L. Mudd

RAMONA L. MUDD

Bloomington, IN

authorHOUSE™

Milton Keynes, UK

Jan 2007

AuthorHouse™
1663 Liberty Drive, Suite 200
Bloomington, IN 47403
www.authorhouse.com
Phone: 1-800-839-8640

AuthorHouse™ UK Ltd.
500 Avebury Boulevard
Central Milton Keynes, MK9 2BE
www.authorhouse.co.uk
Phone: 08001974150

This book is a work of non-fiction. Unless otherwise noted, the author
and the publisher make no explicit guarantees as to the accuracy of
the information contained in this book and in some cases, names of
people and places have been altered to protect their privacy.

First published by AuthorHouse 6/9/2006

ISBN: 1-4259-3783-7 (sc)
ISBN: 1-4259-3784-5 (dj)

Library of Congress Control Number: 2006904413

Printed in the United States of America
Bloomington, Indiana

This book is printed on acid-free paper.

Author's Note:

Seven percent of the author's personal profits are being donated to Global Green USA.
For more information about this organization, visit www.globalgreen.org

Never doubt that a small group of concerned citizens can change the world.
Indeed, it is the only thing that ever has.

~ Margret Mead

For Grandma and Grandpa

Dear Reader,

I have played many roles in my life: daughter, friend, mother, teacher, and wife. I have been described in many ways: fierce, loyal, outgoing, and unfeeling. I have been conflicted: both anxious and arrogant, heartless and charming, funny and bitter. Life has uncovered different shades of my personality at different times. I have been an embarrassment to myself, an inspiration to others, and everything in between.

Who have you been? A provider, a protector, or a guardian angel? Maybe you've been a bad influence? After all, you can't claim to have really lived in your skin until you've known your capacity for great humanity—and acknowledged your ability to also be terribly unkind.

The road to maturity is never-ending, and it's never straight. It is filled with peaks, valleys, harrowing turns, and flat stretches. You pick things up along the way, and drop other things off. But you have been many things, as have I, and you will be much more before it's all over.

As we grow older, we become the person we are meant to be. Having tried on many roles, we know what fits, and what simply doesn't work. I am only thirty-one years old, so the person I am right now is a pale comparison to the person I will be in ten years, or in twenty.

This is only one journey, a collection of the roles I have played. My triumphs, both great and small. My stumbles, from the miserable to the absurd.

Who have you been? Where have you gone? Who will you be?
Find out.

Table of Contents

PART ONE:
THE SCHOOL YEARS

"A woman's life can really be a succession of lives, each revolving around some emotionally compelling situation or challenge, and each marked off by some intense experience."

~Wallis Simpson (1896-1986)
Duchess of Windsor

1

From: Megan
Sent: Wednesday, March 02 2005, 2:41PM
To: Girls
Subject: My, How Times Have Changed

I had recess duty earlier today and thought I had everything under control. Apparently I had WAAYYYY underestimated the mind of a 6th grader…because today, behind a wall of students, two other students were kissing. KISSING! In front of classmates! What was I doing at this age? This is way over my head.

Reply All
From: Amy

Joey Wickman kissed me in Kindergarten. Shane McKenna wrote me a love note in 2nd grade.

Reply All
From: Mona

My first kiss was in the pool around 6th grade, a little peck from a guy named Robby. I wouldn't know him now if he hit me over the head with a frying pan. My first real kiss (and I use that term lightly) was from my beloved Luke Daniels in the 8th grade.

Reply All
From: Lynn

And they say the Catholic girls start much too late.

Reply All
From: Bridget

I got my first kiss in the playhouse in kindergarten by a boy named Josh.
P.S. Megan, what's the protocol for kissing on the playground?

Reply All
From: Amy

Here's my protocol: Make one of them eat a raw clove of garlic and the other some spicy Mexican, then force them to remain lip-locked for a solid 30 minutes.

Reply
From: Bridget

...and that's why Amy's not a teacher.

Reply
From: Cathy

Well I think all you girls are sluts...kissing in grade school. I see now what your private school education got you— TROUBLE! Of course no one would have kissed me prior to 8th grade thanks to my Grade A bucked front teeth...but I'm not bitter.

CHAPTER ONE

I HAVE KNOWN MY FRIEND LYNN for as long as I can remember. We met when I was six years old and she, a mature seven. In my heart she is my sister, and I have no memories of childhood that don't include her.

She and I had been friends and neighbors for four years by the time the Smiths moved in next door to me. I am not making that name up. No, it is not a transparent attempt at a fake last name. Their surname was in fact, Smith. As it happened, the Smiths had a teenage son to their credit. He was as delightful to look at as anyone we had ever seen.

When I look back now, although I cannot call his face to mind, I suspect that he actually was not all that delightful to look at. If teenagers now are any indication, I imagine he was lanky, with unruly limbs, a bit of an acne problem, and wild mood swings. But the cutest boy in our school was Tommy Pastori and our collective future with him didn't look too bright, so we moved on to the new neighbor.

Max was his name. Like a dog.

One afternoon, I came home to find the house empty of its occupants. The far off sounds of laughter and splashing sent me out back to the pool. As I opened the back door and prepared to walk down the steps, I paused, arrested by the sight that greeted me. Max was in the pool and someone else—someone better—was diving off the diving board.

I think the adults around the pool greeted me, but my eyes never left our newest arrival as he resurfaced and shook his hair out of his eyes. Johnny was his name. Max's Cousin Johnny. We were introduced, and I must have said hello. I don't remember. I was staring down at perfection itself, and I'm sure the combination of my hexagonal glasses and fake front tooth—a slightly different color than its partner—stopped him dead in his tracks as well.

Lynn and I soon cooked up a plan to marry them, thereby making us cousins by marriage. By mutual consent, we decided from then on that I would pursue Johnny and she could have Max. After all, Max and I were next door neighbors. We were practically related anyway.

And so it began.

Lynn and I had caught the summer Olympics of the previous year and ever since had fancied ourselves gymnasts in the style of Mary Lou Retton and Mitch Gaylord. Neither of us had ever taken a gymnastics lesson, although I had taken a few sessions of dance. That ended abruptly when I did a kick at a recital that sent my shoe flying into the audience.

Lack of gymnastic training notwithstanding, Lynn and I had taken the swing and seesaw off of her swing set the previous summer. In lieu of the tapes and chalk used by the Olympic hopefuls, we bound our hands with toilet paper and baby powder. Then, hands stiff at our sides, we would run to the bar and leap. In our minds we were spinning, up and up, only to stop poised erect above the bar, muscles quivering and straining with the effort. We performed any number of imaginary gymnastic feats, and jumped off. Sticking the ending to secure a Perfect 10.

Since Max moved in, we moved our recital from her back yard to mine. I didn't have a swing set, so we turned our attention to the floor exercise. We placed our mat, a floral quilt rescued from the cedar chest, under the oak trees in my backyard. This provided us with shade— and an unobstructed view of the Smith's sunroom. Daily, we worked to perfect our round-off-back-handspring-twist segment. This, to the untrained eye, may have appeared to be a handstand followed by a cartwheel, then wrapped up with a somersault. That was dicey because of the acorns, but we had a man to catch. Sprains be damned!

Max rarely ventured out of his house, and if he did, never came over and talked to us—thus sparing us the necessity of forming a coherent sentence, and sparing him our unfortunate tendency to giggle.

Over the years, I have wondered what we were thinking. Was there a chance he would come over and watch us? Perhaps he would come jogging out of his house one day, clipboard in one hand, more baby powder in the other? Secretly, we imagined him staring at us out his kitchen window talking to his cousin on the phone. "You should see their flips!" He would say. "They simply defy gravity!" Then Johnny would come cruising over on his Huffy to see what all the fuss was about.

As a child, the last time I saw Johnny I was eleven. Right before it got out that I lied to some of my classmates and told them he was my boyfriend. I was forced to concede that a boy, who actually hid when I was around, was not interested in me. However, I did see him a few years back; had a college class with him. He didn't recognize me at first, but when I introduced myself—I don't think I imagined his step backwards. As for Lynn, her infatuation with Max ended the day he broke her heart. He stepped off the school bus, arm around a little blonde girl, and kissed her right there at the curb.

In the following years, Lambert-St. Louis International Airport bought out our neighborhood to create a buffer zone for its expansion. Lynn moved about thirty miles away, across the river. My mom married and we moved to a neighboring town. The last time Lynn and I went back, the three trees that stood in my backyard were still there. So were the pines that marched along the back of her parents' property.

The houses are all gone. The pool where we swam our summers away has been filled in. The wintry hills of her backyard have been leveled. But I like that the trees are still there. And if our childhood selves can inhabit a place where, as adults, we can no longer go, I imagine that a part of me and a part of Lynn are still running wild among those trees, laughing and flipping in the wind.

As luck would have it, Lynn and I did grow up to marry cousins, ensuring that we see each other on all the major holidays. But, as you may have guessed, they aren't this set of cousins.

From: Megan
Sent: Monday, April 04, 2005 2:55 PM
To: Girls

Am I the only one who finds it really creepy that they are parading the Pope's body around in the streets?
No coffin, no containment whatsoever, just displayed on a 'bed.'
Yuck.

Reply All
From: Mona

Yes. I'm sure there's some deeper meaning attached that has been passed down through the ages, but after 13 solid years of Catholic school, I find that I have no idea what it is, so I was also...disoriented—to say the least—by the day's events. But what can you say? Damn Europeans.

Reply All
From: Amy

I think its part of his lifelong commitment to being accessible the people. Quite a man, that one.
PS. Note the "blistering sun" description we keep hearing. Double yuck.

Reply All
From: Cathy

Oh, don't get me started...Poor Prince Charles has had to postpone his wedding to go to Rome. I'm sure the Royals are bummed. I hope they get all their deposits back from the wedding vendors.

Reply All
From: Christian

You guys are disgusting.

Reply All
From: Mona

Well, yeah. It doesn't take us long to abandon the first five stages of grief and set up camp in the sixth and seventh. Disrespect and Sacrilege.

Chapter Two

I don't mind telling you that, in grade school, I was a bit of a nerd.

My mom and I lived with my grandparents. Mom left pretty early for work, so it fell to my grandma—the least domestic person on the planet—to fix my hair in the mornings. She solved that problem by braiding my hair or rolling it in curlers the night before school, then sliding a pair of her pantyhose on top of my head before sending me to bed. And to make a bad thing worse, I had glasses—which was just about the only fashion choice you couldn't get away with in the Eighties. I had really lousy self-esteem, so I probably wasn't as much of an outcast as I perceived that I was, but the offers of friendship weren't rolling in, either. Theresa Owens was the only friend I had in my class, although I remained on friendly, if vague, terms with everyone else. They didn't often invite me over for sleepovers, but neither did they corner me in the parking lot after school. I'd like to tell you that, together, Theresa and I took our unlikely friendship and marched straight to the top of the heap, but that didn't happen. Rather, we were outcasts together, instead of individually, and provided each other with the only thing that really mattered in school: somebody to sit by in the cafeteria.

We made it through grade school relatively unscathed, but pursued separate paths after graduation. She had been accepted to Incarnate Word Academy, a prestigious all girls school. And in the fall of 1988, I started St. Thomas Aquinas-Mercy High School.

Lynn had begun high school the year before, and was already mapping out her chosen path for me once I joined her there. Her first priority was convincing me to try out for the cheerleading squad, and since she had a persuasive way about her that I never bothered to resist, I followed her lead.

As a result of her machinations, by my junior year, I managed a modicum of high school level celebrity. Which, of course, did me no good in the real world, but it did make those four years a little less hellish.

My classes covered a wide range, from the general level to the advanced, so I had the benefit of knowing every single person in my class rather than a limited cross-section. I had Mass Media with the motor head crowd. An intimidating group, yes, but they patiently answered all of my questions about chassis, timing belts, and brake pads.

I had Language Arts with a malicious group of girls who took me under their wing because they thought I should be "meaner." The burnouts and I had a grand old time in American History, and most of the football team was in my religion class. I didn't pay much attention, though. I was too concerned about Lori, who sat in front of me and flipped her hair onto my desk on a daily basis. She thought it was beautiful. I thought it had the consistency of cellophane.

"Father Cooper? Do you have a pair of scissors?" I would ask loudly. And often.

The Bridgets laughed every time. They sat, one in front of the other, in the row along the window. Then, my boyfriend, Jack, would lean over to search his pile of belongings, and say something like, "I have a glue stick."

"That'll work. Give it to me."

Then Lori would shoot us all a hateful look, which never failed to make my day, and would have made the girls in Language Arts so proud.

From Religion class, I went to lunch, and afterward I got to spend time with a whole new crop of people. My smart friends.

"Hey!"

A pencil eraser hit my hand the same time Dale whispered to me across the aisle. I had been slowly chewing my contraband gum and inspecting my hair for split ends. I shifted to seat myself more comfortably on one foot and threw my ponytail over my shoulder.

"*What?*" I mouthed my response.

Dale and I were sitting in Advanced Algebra one afternoon, biding our time through an endless round of questions from another classmate, Molly, to our teacher. I have since heard that she became an accountant, or something, which explains why she asked questions in math class like her life depended on understanding the answer.

I didn't look at Dale. To do so would give away our inattention, and you didn't talk in Mrs. Wendell's class. She liked to throw erasers. You couldn't start your homework either, because she was a sadist and wouldn't give out the assignment until everyone fully understood the lesson, and Molly was relentless in her quest for mastery.

"But how did you get $3x$ over 7, on the left side of the equation?"

Like terms! I wanted to cry. *She's combining like terms. Come on!*

Dale folded his lanky frame and bent to pick up his eraser. "You going to the game tonight?" He asked on the way down.

I looked at him, then at my cheerleading uniform. "Uh, I'm cheering it, so I guess so…"

From the front of the room, Molly asked, "Okay. So then why did you divide by two?" and I briefly considered banging my head on my desk until I lost consciousness. Dale pulled a face. "What's your problem?"

"Nothing!" I snapped distractedly, and glanced at him. "Sorry."

Soon, Mrs. Wendell was free to review the final part of the lesson, which she did while wandering aimlessly on our side of the room. Conversation was momentarily stalled, an outcome that was anything but coincidence, I'm sure. As she spoke, I listened to the faint whistle of the radiator and the miscellaneous sounds of boredom in the classroom. Dale stared at the teacher in mock absorption, following her every move, and nodding in constant agreement.

"What are we doing afterward?" I asked when she began the return trip to her desk.

"Mona! Quiet!" Mrs. Wendell barked in warning.

Damn.

"And spit out your gum!"

Damn again.

I leaned back and threw it away, then wrote on my notebook, "*What's going on after the game?*"

"*Charlie's having people over,*" he answered on his paper bag book cover.

Mrs. Wendell had reached her desk and was performing some mysterious teacher rituals while we waited. She scratched a reminder in pencil on a Post-it note. She flipped the pages of her teacher's guide. Back, and forth. Back, and forth. When she reached into her desk drawer, I leaned toward Dale.

"I can go. Well, I'll ask Amy, she's driving." I drummed my pencil in thought. "Jack won't be there. He has a family thing."

"I know. He told me to watch you—"

I stopped my drumming. *Watch me?* "What for?"

"I don't know." He shrugged one shoulder. "Says you'll get away from him if I don't—"

"Excuse me," interrupted a cold voice from the front of the room, and my offense at Jack's high-handedness gave way to abject fear. I looked toward Mrs. Wendell and caught her staring in our direction.

A quick glance around the room confirmed she had been at it for a while.

"If Mona and Dale are ready, I'll tell you your homework assignment."

Dale jumped to defend himself. "I'm sorry, Mrs. Wendell. Mona won't stop talking." He looked at me. "I keep telling you, 'Stop talking. I'm listening to the teacher,' but you—"

Whack!

Dale's lecture was interrupted by a chalkboard eraser. It slapped the wall behind his head, showering him with a fine white film of dust, and landed on the floor at his feet.

Mrs. Wendell hid a smile and pitched her voice over the amusement traveling around the room.

"Now that I've got your attention, let's talk about tonight's homework…"

When I exited the room ten minutes later, someone grabbed my hand and pulled me from the crowd of departing students. I was spun into a nearby bay of lockers.

"I haven't seen you yet today." Jack lightly pulled my hair. "Cute ponytail."

I leaned back on the cold metal. He smelled delicious. Like clean clothes and cold air. His hair was still damp from the shower.

"Where have you been?"

"Overslept," he shrugged, with the confidence of a guy who could forge a tardy slip.

"It's one o'clock in the afternoon...Quit!" I swatted him away as he moved to untie the yellow ribbon in my hair. "Hey. What's this about Dale 'watching me' tonight?"

He chuckled lightly to himself.

"What?" My anger escalated with his laughter. "What's so funny?"

A freshman opened his locker down the way. Jack smiled dimly at him and I scooted further to the side in a bid for privacy.

His voice took on a distracted quality. "God... this bow thing is so cute on you..."

"Hey!" I persisted and smacked him on the chest. "I'm really mad at you."

Finally, he focused on me. "Why? Can't I have someone keep an eye on my girl?"

I challenged him with a lift of my chin. "I'm not your girl."

"Oh, really?" He scratched his chin as if he was thinking. "See... that's not how I remember it..."

I hugged my math book to my chest, and geared myself for battle. "What's *that* supposed to mean?" I shot back.

Abruptly, he seemed to lose interest in fighting with me. He smiled at me then, in the way he always did. A little bit charmed. A little bit tired.

"Nothing."

I regretted my hasty words. But before I could apologize, he leaned down and kissed me. Quick. Efficient. A reminder. Then he was gone. I was left standing, alone. All of my comebacks aborted, and all of my anger turned inward.

I made my way, slowly, down the empty hallway. Sorry. Confused. And late for English Literature.

From: Amy
Sent: Thursday, February 03, 2005 12:08 PM
To: Mona
Subject: Did you know?

Spell check for Mona Mudd suggests Mohammad. So I will be expecting great things from you.

Reply
From: Mona

You'll be waiting a while.

CHAPTER THREE

FOR HALF OF MY SOPHOMORE AND all of my junior year of high school, I dated Jack. For reasons known to me now but too lengthy to explain, I repeatedly broke up with him, and probably would have gone on doing so indefinitely. However, our senior year he turned the tables and broke up with me. So ensued ten months of pain and anguish as I tried over and over to get him back, and he appeared to consider it over and over until he ultimately decided against it.

An otherwise unremarkable day in October of 1991 found us on the football field. We were doing a practice run of Friday's Pep Rally, which was designed to present the Homecoming Court as well as build excitement for Saturday's Homecoming Game. I had been elected to the Homecoming Court earlier in the week and had to pick a soccer player to escort me during the Pep Rally. In a stunning display of masochism, I asked Jack. In an equally stunning bit of stupidity, he accepted.

It was just our luck that earlier in the day Jack had refused to take me back—for about the fourth time. I believed him this time more than most because he had gone as far as breaking our plans for the Homecoming Dance. Having failed to sway him with a little strategy

I like to call "begging," I resorted to spite, somehow thinking that would change his mind.

"Are you going with someone else?" This I asked while we were walking to our places.

Jack squinted into the sun and attempted a smile for appearance's sake. "No Mona..."

My friend Amy was also on the Court, and she watched us warily as we passed.

"Who is she?" I asked, as I sent a placating smile Amy's way.

She narrowed her eyes in curiosity. After years of friendship, I knew her concern rested halfway between the possibility that I was going to make a scene, and the inevitability of it.

Jack made a frustrated sound. Bitter and ugly. "You're amazing, you know that? You broke up with me a thousand times, and I break up with you *once* and I get a guilt trip!" –which, of course, was beside the point. I wasn't mad that he broke up with me. I was mad that he wouldn't come back.

As soon as we found our spot, we both turned and focused our attention forward.

"Is it Lisa or Missy?" I persisted. "It's tough to tell who you like these days, the way you hang all over anybody."

He sent me a disgusted glance. Lately I could have started a collection.

"Screw you," he responded.

"Oh that's clever, Jack. Well said." I began a short round of applause. "Bravo!"

Jack ignored me, and Amy's expression turned thunderous.

"Mona and Jack. Now, you two step forward." Mr. Palmer, the English teacher, was all business.

I stopped clapping to loop my hand in the crook of his arm, and he took advantage of my silence to go on in a nasty undertone. "I'm surprised you haven't come to my window lately telling me how desperately you love me."

I narrowed my eyes at his profile. He knew how I regretted that little episode, yet he still threw it back in my face.

"Hey," he reminded me, "I'll probably be asleep around one o'clock in the morning, if you want to come over and wake me up again."

"Oh shut up." I was pretty eloquent myself.

He mocked me with a thumbs-up. "Hey! Good one!"

From the front of the field, Mr. Palmer said, "Jack, walk Mona slowly forward, then turn to the right."

"God, I hate you," I hissed and as we were walking to our place.

Jack gave a rueful little laugh devoid of any amusement. "You love me. You hate me. You love me. You hate me…but if I put any effort into it at all you'd—" Before he could finish the sentence, his head snapped back and to the left. To this day, I don't know for sure how he was going to complete that thought, but I had a pretty good idea. I couldn't bear for him to be that mean of a person, so I punched him. Right in the face.

I've never punched anybody else in my life, though I've been sorely tempted, so I can't say what it was that came over me that day. All I can say in my defense was—at the time—it seemed to be a good idea. But a minute later, it lost some of its appeal.

Jack's reaction was to shove me. Hard. "You make me sick!"

I went stumbling backwards. He truly wasn't a violent person, but then neither was I. We were both simply reduced to a point where we brought out the worst in each other.

The ground was slick from that morning's rain, so my feet slipped as I fought to keep my balance. My hip caught the brunt of my fall, and I rolled to a sitting position. I glanced up from my inspection of my hip and elbow to see him checking the corner of his lip for blood.

He was furious. "You are pathetic! Do you know that?"

"Jack, I…"

"You call me all hours of the night crying…you come to my house…" And on he went—every word a blow to me, sharp and perfectly aimed. I sat on the damp ground, too ashamed to look at him again, and absorbed every bit of it.

The worst part was that he spoke nothing but the truth. I had a million excuses for myself—for my behavior—but they were just that: excuses. It was one of the moments in my life when everything came into focus. I thought of every time I pulled him out of class because I was upset. Every time I tried to intimidate the girls he wanted to date. Every time I called in the middle of the night. And I admitted it, if only to myself. I *was* pathetic.

I finally looked up at him and he shook his head. "God, I don't even want to look at you anymore..."

As I turned to watch him leave, I noticed other people on the field in varying degrees of proximity. As if they had wanted to help, but only ended up frozen and eavesdropping—which wasn't difficult considering that Jack had been shouting most of his lines. I couldn't fault them. I loved gossip as much as the next person. If I'd had the pleasure of being a witness, rather than a participant, I'm not sure I would have been able to reign in my excitement. Jack's friend Dale was nearest to me, and sprang into motion when I started to rise. He tried to help me up, but I waved off his assistance. "I'm fine." Then I walked off the football field by myself. Past the stares, the curious looks, and the hidden smiles of a few. No one called us back. Not even Mr. Palmer.

On that Saturday, my dad and I were in much the same positions as Jack and I had been on Thursday afternoon, but without the glaring hostility. That was just the way it went. Soccer players escorted the members of the Homecoming Court during Friday afternoon's Pep Rally. Fathers escorted their daughters during Saturday's Homecoming Game when the queen was announced. And football players escorted them when they were presented during the Homecoming Dance on Saturday night.

When my name was announced as Homecoming Queen that afternoon, I was surprised and genuinely touched, but emotionally I was a shipwreck. As it happened, the voice on the loudspeaker said: "The Class of 1992 Homecoming Queen is… Mona Chevalier…" and a giant roar went up in the crowd.

Before I was ambushed by the wall of people running my way, my dad leaned over and said, "Looks like you have quite a following here at school." He stepped back, and then ran for cover.

After all the congratulations were over, I headed toward the gym for a soda. When I was rounding the corner, I saw Jack. He was alone, leaning against a black metal rail watching my approach. I slowly walked over, and stood in front of him. He refused to look at me for an interminable length of time, and then he flicked his gaze over my face.

"Congratulations," he said in a low voice, then shifted his focus back to the crowd in the distance.

I lowered my gaze, and became obsessed with rolling a nearby pebble beneath my shoe. I still wanted him to go to the dance with me, but even in my desperate state, I could see that it wouldn't magically transform us back to the way we had been.

"I know we can't go together tonight…" I glanced up and saw him issue a short, wordless nod. Then he settled his gaze on the asphalt at my feet. "….but I still wish we could, you know?"

"I wish we could too," he admitted. Then he moved his head up and down, as if agreeing with himself.

I took a breath. "Then why —"

"Don't." He raised a staying hand to block my words. "Okay? For once… just…don't."

The air backed up in my lungs at his tone. It warned me that he was, perhaps, as far away from happiness as I was at the moment. So in a rare—and fleeting—moment of empathy, I didn't push the issue. I looked around, aware of our surroundings for the first time, as if someone had abruptly turned up the volume. Students, teachers, and parents were milling around us, most of them unaware of our little drama that was unfolding. But some were casting glances in our direction with mingled expressions of horror, sadness, and glee that they just might witness Round Two.

I started to say something else. Make some flippant comment to ease the tension, but I couldn't think of anything to say. I tried to smile, to let people know that we were okay. But we weren't, and I didn't have the energy to put on a show that day.

Suddenly, I had to get away. Without another word I turned toward the gym doors.

Five...four...

Once in the gym, I ran for the solitude of the bathroom.

Three...

Locked myself in the furthest stall.

Two...One—

"Mona!" Amy barged in. Jack had probably sent her in after me. At the time, I convinced myself it meant he still cared. Now I realize he was just sick of cleaning up the mess that was Me.

"Where are you?" She yelled.

"...in here."

Her rubber soled shoes marched across the cheap linoleum. She rattled the stall door. "Open up."

When I did, she squeezed her way in the door and shut it behind her. I was sitting on the bathroom floor—an indication of how insane with grief I was. Never in my right mind would I sit on the floor of a public restroom.

"Oh, Mona," she breathed, more to herself than me. Then she leaned over and scraped her palms down my wet cheeks. We sat in silence for a moment. All at once, she decided on a plan of action. "You just need to block it out." Leaning forward, she swatted and pulled at the toilet paper roll. "Here." She stuffed a pile of tissue in my hand and pulled me to my feet.

"What?" I didn't understand what she meant. She seemed to be talking too fast. Moving too fast. All I wanted to do was sit, and never come out of the bathroom again.

"Block it out," she explained. "Forget he's here. Don't look at him, don't listen for him..." She turned and looked me straight in the eye. "You cannot fall apart right now. You know that, right?" Then she opened the stall door. "You've got a Homecoming game to cheer, and half-time's almost over."

I grabbed the tissue and followed her over to the sinks. "No, you don't understand, Amy, I can't go out there..."

The feeling was too overwhelming, too frightening. The idea that I couldn't make him want me anymore was new to me. It was heartbreaking. It was horrible. And it was insulting.

"Well, you don't have a choice."

I headed back to the stall in response, but she grabbed my arm.

"Amy!" I wrenched my arm free. "You're not listening! I cannot go out there and pretend to be happy—"

28

"You have to."

"Why?"

She didn't answer.

"Why?"

I motioned in the general direction of the football stands. "For them? Is the whole school going to fall apart if I don't look happy right now?!"

"No!" She finally yelled. "No they're not! Because, you know what? The whole damn world does not revolve around how *Mona* is feeling today!"

I stared at her in shock. I had never seen that side of Amy. She was usually very patient with my wild swings of emotion, but there will come a moment in some friendships when you've exhausted every avenue of compassion. I knew in that moment that Amy was tired of me.

She pointed toward the door, and continued on. "That crowd out there wants to see their Homecoming Queen. And they want to see her happy. And grateful. When you get home, you cry your eyes out if you want to, but do *not* do this now!"

I glared at her in the silence. She glared back.

"Fine!" I said and snatched the cool cloth she held out to me. I held it on my eyes to reduce the puffiness, then she handed me her lip gloss.

"Put some of this on."

I obeyed. What else could I do? She had become a force to be reckoned with.

Finally, we walked to the door. Before Amy opened it, she turned and issued one last command.

"Now, I'm going to open this door. Smile. Or I'll kill you."

That night, I went to the dance with my girlfriends. I was in a daze, lost in my thoughts. I smiled when I was supposed to and laughed when it was expected, but I don't remember much.

Our song that year was "Everything I Do" by Bryan Adams. When it came on, I walked up to Jack and asked him to dance.

He shook his head slowly and refused.

I spoke past the lump in my throat. "Why not?"

"I'm not gonna be the one to make you cry tonight."

I wanted to cry, to beg, to do something—anything—to have him back. But instead I only nodded. He was right. If given the slightest chance, I would have lost what fragile control I had over myself.

A hundred other couples were dancing on the floor that night. But I stood rooted in one spot, with a crown on my head, watching him walk away.

From: Stagner
Sent: Monday, January 16, 2006 12:47 PM
To: Amy; Bridget; Megan; Mona; Christian
Subject: Don't forget to vote

ok...this is too funny......my poor sister. You guys have to get on the fox sports website and cast your vote. Neil has made it to the finals for sexiest man in the NFL. He's up against Brett Favre. That will be really funny if he wins. My brother-in-law! Ha!

Reply All
From: Mona

Listen, here missy...
I'm quite sure I can't possibly vote Neil Rakers as the sexiest man in the NFL...since I can barely picture him above the age of 14, over at Bridget's house, hanging out with her brother Mike. Although I will vote him this:
"Sexiest-Man-To-Stand-On-The-Sidelines-And-Drink-With-During-Your-Wedding-Since-We-Were-Only-Readers-And-Therefore-Not- Needed-For-Any-Of-The-Pictures"

Reply
From: Stagner

Hey! I took a picture of you guys!

CHAPTER FOUR

SOMEBODY WROTE A BOOK ONCE, AND claimed that everything we ever really needed to know we learned in Kindergarten. I would agree—in part. Everything I ever really needed to know *about being nice,* I did learn in Kindergarten.

But what of our negative social skills? Where do those come from?

Well, I picked mine up in high school.

To be fair, I learned more positive lessons than negative, which I think makes me luckier than most. But that's the thing about negative experiences—they're painful. So, they tend to stick with you.

During my freshman year, I learned how to break up with someone and survive the vicious fall-out. By sophomore year, I knew how to ignore someone until they apologized, and how to cover my embarrassment by being the one who always laughs first. Some time during junior year, I perfected the fine art of ignoring someone outwardly while, at the same time, being completely aware of their every movement.

And for all of my senior year, I got to hone my ability to appear happy, while actually being the furthest thing from it. I knew exactly how to use charm, sarcasm, and humor to manipulate just about every situation to my advantage.

Except for one.

In early spring of 1992, Jack had a party at his house. I had just won a game of pool against him and we were arguing about it—which was no big surprise—we would argue about the color of the grass back then.

Somehow, in the course of all our dramatics, we developed a tentative friendship. Jack was enjoying himself too much to be tied down. I recognized that, and had lost interest in the person he had become, even as I still longed for the boy he once was.

Later in the night, I ran upstairs to use the restroom. The one in the hall was occupied, so I headed for the one in Jack's parent's room. A few minutes later, I opened the door to return to the party, and ran headlong into Jack.

I raised a hand to my galloping heartbeat. "Oh! You scared me!"

"Sorry." He grinned in apology. "Someone's in the other bathroom."

"Well, I'm done in here." I started to scoot past him when he grabbed my arm.

"Hang on a second, will you?"

A few moments later, he spoke to me through the partially closed door. "You know, I was thinking about what Bridget said."

My head snapped up from the picture I was looking at. Earlier in the evening, Bridget and Jack had been discussing the idea that he and I should get back together. I wasn't part of the conversation, as is often the case in high school, when the person truly in charge of your destiny is your best friend. I heard snippets of it from my position three feet away, and had latched onto them like they were a raft and I was a drowning man. But standing in his parent's room, it seemed a good idea to feign ignorance.

"What'd she say?"

Jack turned out the light in the bathroom and walked toward me as he tucked in his shirt. "You know, that we need to do something about our relationship."

My quiet laugh broke the silence. "That's funny." I turned for the door.

He trailed behind me. "What's so funny about it?"

"Well, Jack," I said over my shoulder, "there's nothing *to* do. When we date, we do nothing but fight. Besides, you're dating somebody now."

Somebody was a sophomore who was just about the cutest thing going for the class of '94. I frequently dreamed of the day she'd break her nose or perhaps lose a tooth. But none of those things ever happened and she remained sweet and fresh-faced.

Jack interrupted my thoughts by saying, "We're not serious," which had disaster written all over it.

I made it as far as the hall, when he used his body to railroad me into his room. He followed me in and slammed the door.

"I want to kiss you." *Wow! This was sudden...well, maybe not.*

He persisted, "Do you want to kiss me?"

"No." Yes.

"You're a bad liar." He took a step forward. I took one back.

"Jack, you don't even like me anymore." He was advancing still, and I was looking anywhere but at him.

"What if I told you I did? That I have all along?"

I glanced behind me to check my progress. "I wouldn't believe you."

"Why not?" Another step forward.

"Because you've been drinking, and you always say that kind of stuff when you've been drinking."

"Maybe everything I've been trying to hide just comes out when I'm drinking," he suggested.

"Yes. I've heard that..." *Smack.* I ran into the wall. "...happens."

I shook my head. "We can't do this."

"But we want to."

I slammed my hands on his chest to stop his approach. "Well, that's not really the point—"

He grabbed my hands and flung them to the side. "I'm sorry," was all he said before he reached in, grabbed my face and kissed me.

It was wonderful. It was terrible. But we couldn't stop. In between, we kept apologizing to each other. *I'm sorry. I'm sorry. I'm sorry.* For what, we didn't know, but we knew we were sorry. That we would be sorry.

When he reached for my shirt I pushed him away. "Please stop."

He pulled away, uttering a low curse as he sat heavily on the edge of his bed. He rubbed his forehead with the heels of his hands, and I remember wondering if he was trying to scrub his thoughts into order.

I was leaning over with my hands on my knees trying to regain my equilibrium, both physically and emotionally. Eventually I pulled myself together and stood. "Okay, this is stupid."

"I don't want to keep hurting you but I do," he said to the floor.

"Jack, I'm fine," I said. But I wasn't. Oh how I wasn't.

Dale came barging in the room, "Hey, sorry for interrupting..."

He didn't interrupt anything, and he looked mighty disappointed about that fact, too. Never let it be said that I didn't answer when opportunity knocked. I fled.

"Hold on, Dale," I heard Jack say as he followed me into the hallway.

"We have to talk."

I kept walking, my back to him. "No, we don't."

"Mona." He sidled past me and blocked my progress.

I stopped. "Fine. What should we talk about?"

"This!" He answered, gesturing back and forth between us.

"What are you talking about?" I mimicked his movement. "What is *this*? Is it this thing where you can't make up your mind?"

Jack got angry then. "You won't fight for me at all will you?"

"What? Fight *you* for you?"

He didn't answer.

"You're crazy," I accused, and started move around him, then stopped, suddenly furious. "No! You know what? You want to do all of this your way. You want to see what's out there, but you want me waiting for you to come back to!" I punctuated my accusations by shoving him in the chest. "Let's talk about that!"

At my words, he threw his hands in the air in frustration. "Mona, it's not like that—"

"Yes it is!" I shouted over him. "You have no idea how hard this is for me!"

"Oh I don't?" He stepped right up in my face. "Did you forget all the times you were 'confused' last year and I waited around for you?"

"Jesus! How many times do I have to pay for that?"

"I don't know Mona," he yelled. "Let me think, how many times did you break up with me?" He began ticking them off on his fingers. "Two weeks after we first got together. After you saw me talking to that girl at Charlie's party. After the swimming party at Bridget's. When you met that guy Tim in Driver's Ed. And my personal favorite, after I took you out for your birthday!" He shouted the last word in emphasis, although it was unnecessary. I got it, loud and clear.

I was stunned. "So that's it?"

Jack, horrified, held out a hand in entreaty, stammering in his attempt to backpedal. "No…Wait…I'm sorry." He put his hands up in surrender, and stepped to the side to block my retreat. "That's not why I'm doing this, that's not what I meant."

I stared at the empty space between us, "So I deserve this?"

"No, Mona." His hands fell down to his sides. "Nobody deserves this."

Looking back, I should have stopped there. There was probably a real chance to mend fences at that point, but my feelings were hurt. Worse, we had drawn an audience and my pride was on the line.

"Don't worry about it, Jack." I snapped, "You won't even remember this in the morning."

He flinched as if I had slapped him. I pushed past him, and grabbed my purse off of the couch. The last thing I saw before I slammed out of the door was him standing motionless, right where I had left him.

After that night, a rift arose that we could not bridge. I was disappointed in myself. In him. And I can't claim to know anything of his feelings.

At that time, I developed and understanding for that thin line between love and hate. I felt sorry for the people caught in the middle of our adolescent battles. We still hung around the same group of people, so those in the middle were our friends. People reluctant to choose any real side.

"Mona. You guys have got to stop this."

Bridget and I were sitting outside during our unstructured class period. She was trying to talk some sense into me—which was a part-time gig at the time, but in the following years would become her full-time job.

I remained adamant. "We will. When he apologizes."

Bridget closed her eyes and, I imagine, prayed for patience. "Mona," she began again, "I know he shouldn't have said that about you breaking up with him so many times." She held up an index finger to stop my response. "*But...* maybe you were a little hard on him too."

I was incredulous. "When?"

"Uh... How 'bout when you said he wouldn't remember it in the morning because he was so drunk?"

I waved a dismissing hand. "Oh, who knew he'd actually remember..."

"But the point is that he did! And it hurt him a lot."

"Well, the truth hurts."

"Mona! You are deliberately missing the point." She took a deep, calming breath. "Okay. Just let me say this—"

I rolled my eyes.

"—would you just listen? Please?"

"Yes!" I snapped. "What?"

She gave me a look of warning. You didn't snap at Bridget.

"Sorry," I muttered.

She nodded. "It's okay. But what I was saying was…maybe just consider the idea that you both might have been a little bit wrong. And you both were a little bit right."

I shrugged half-heartedly. "Maybe."

She put her arm around my shoulders and softened her voice.

"You gonna be okay?"

I sat there silently. When I had beaten the tears back, I lifted my face.

"It'll all be over soon," she said, by way of cheering me up. "I know it sucks, Mona, but sometimes you just gotta get through it..." she added. But her voice seemed to fade away to nothing.

The sun mocked my mood, but even I had to admit it was a beautiful day. Warm and bright, with a just a touch of leftover winter in the breeze. We sat there lost in our thoughts for what could have been a minute, or could have been an hour. I watched a bird flit from limb to limb on a nearby holly bush and Bridget's expression was far, far away.

When Graduation finally came, my relief was palpable. Finally I didn't have to see him anymore. I didn't have to hear him, or catch the scent of him. There was an end in sight. After months of rolling, nauseating emotion, I had finally found refuge in a completely numb state of being. Never was I very happy, but I didn't feel particularly sad either.

After the ceremony, I found myself walking alone down the steps of the New Cathedral in St. Louis. I told myself not to look back, but of course I did anyway.

Don't we all?

Jack and his new girlfriend were standing with each other, and their families, taking pictures. For a split second, a memory of us doing that very same thing flashed across my mind. I stopped, choked by a welling of regret I thought I had conquered.

Eventually I looked away, and blinked until my vision was clear again. Then I turned around, and took the first step of many in my journey away from him.

The last time I saw Jack was at our ten-year class reunion. He told me right before the evening ended that, "none of that high school stuff mattered," with which I completely disagreed. "Especially all that stuff at the end," he added, and I marveled that after all these years, he still had the power to hurt my feelings.

To hear him say it like that made me sad, and mostly for him. If that's his take on it, then fine. But it mattered to me then, and it still matters to me today. It mattered that I learned I couldn't play with people's emotions. It mattered that I learned to hold on to the people I love most, not push them away. It even mattered that I discovered I was capable of feeling that much pain, because it made me real in a way that I never had been before. And even if the pain took my breath away from time to time, I would still never exchange him, or the memories I have of him. Would never say they didn't matter.

Because young or old—forever, or for just right now—shouldn't every kind of love be that overwhelming? Even all the stuff at the end? And if it's easy to close that door and open a new one, then didn't you miss the point?

PART TWO:
JOINING THE WORKFORCE

"I like living.

I have sometimes been wildly, despairingly, acutely miserable…but through it all I still know quite certainly that just to be alive is a grand thing."

~Agatha Christie (1890-1976)
British writer

From: Amy
Sent: May 27, 2004 9:34 AM
To: Girls, Matt
Subject: Amy's Window

*Traffic is gridlocked in Downtown St. Louis. I'm looking
out my office window down on Memorial Drive. They are
the same cars that were there 10 minutes ago. Poor people.
Stuck in traffic. Sat in it myself on my 7 mile commute- of
which the last ¼ mile took 25 minutes, thanks to two different
accidents at downtown intersections. Like most of my fellow
commuters I sat, cursing at the woman in front of me who
would NOT move through the green light despite plenty of
room on the other side, and the selfish bastard who parked at
the meter in front of my building effectively blocking an entire
lane that could have helped keep people moving – especially
me right into my garage.*
*Then I get in, mention the travails to Tracy who had been
here for an hour and missed the hoo-ha and she said, "You
know what I think of on days like that- those people (in the
totaled cars) are having a much worse day than I am."*

This has been today's edition of Outside Amy's Window

Reply All
From: Cathy

*Greetings from Hot-Lanta, GA! The home of David Sedaris'
guitar teacher.*
*Okay, people like Tracy with their rosy ideas should all
be gathered up and shipped to an island where they can
exchange their happy go lucky thoughts all day long without
bothering the rest of humanity. I'll be heading back to
Arkansas this week. And what shall greet me upon my return*

45

you ask? Well, this week is the Annual Shareholders Meeting.

Reply All
From: Lynn

I'm sure that will be quite the spectacle.

Reply All
From: Mona

Oh, how I always wished I could attend! Every year about this time I sat at the morning meeting, crossed my fingers and prayed, prayed, prayed that somebody important would choose me to represent ... no ... wait... that wasn't me.

From: Matt
Sent: May 27, 2004 10:52 PM
To: Cathy
Cc: Girls

Well Cat, I'm sure you're sound asleep dreaming about your big drive back north. As you drive remember it's probably a journey many slaves took to win a freedom they were willing to die for. So if the drive seems long—just remember—you don't have to do it by the light of a lantern with "the man" and some bloodhounds on your trail. It's all mind over matter. I am going to get ready for bed now, and as I lay my head down to rest, I too will think about my journey tomorrow. Crossing over the Mighty Mississippi remembering settlers that once waved in steamboats bringing valuable goods (perhaps medicine) to their banks. I will smile with respect as I spot a hawk mid-flight before it swoops down, with a precision given only by God to capture a delectable fish...oh who am I kidding...I'll be cursing some imbecile in a mini-van with his "AM in the PM" bumper sticker and his Jack-in-the-Box antenna ball that mocks me as I tail too close wishing why, oh why, when they built this damn bridge didn't they put shoulders on it so I could attempt an illegal pass.

CHAPTER FIVE

IN THE LATTER MONTHS OF **1993,** I got a job at a Wholesale Club with Lynn. We gave out free food samples at our little square tables. We never aspired to be particularly good at it, and as a result, we weren't. I refused to respond to overused comments like: "Hey. What's for lunch?" And Lynn took to answering the observation: "This is cold." with "It's also free."

Eventually we moved up the company ladder, which didn't mean we got paid any more, it just meant more things were our fault. By 1999, Lynn was working part-time in Groceries while going to school for Respiratory Therapy. I worked in the back of the store, unloading tractor-trailers in the Receiving Department. It was there that I met Ronnie Miller.

"I think I'm getting one more tattoo."

Ronnie and I were sitting at the table in the upstairs break room—the smoker's lounge—eating lunch and watching television. Occasionally we were joined by other employees just beginning their workdays, but most of the time it was just the two of us. The rest of our department sat in the downstairs break room, content with their clean lungs and self-righteousness.

I blew on my forkful of chicken and, without looking away from the Showcase Showdown, asked, "What'd you say?" Of course, I had heard Ronnie's pronouncement. I was just buying myself more time to add the price of a Chevy Blazer and a trip to Switzerland in my head.

"A tattoo. I'm getting one more on my shoulder blade," he patted his left shoulder. "Then that's it."

Turning my attention from the television, I challenged him. "Let me get this straight. You're t—" I paused, while someone was paged over the loudspeaker. Then began again.

"You're telling me you're only getting one more tattoo?"

"Yes."

Unconvinced, I persisted. "Forever?"

"Yes."

"You expect me to believe that?"

He nodded. "That's right."

I leaned forward, my lunch momentarily forgotten. "In the time I've known you, you've gotten three tattoos. Yet somehow you are going to stick to just *one* more for the next fifty or so years?"

At a loss for an answer, he ignored the question. The only indication he heard me was his faint grin.

I sat there taking in his appearance as he lit a cigarette. Everything from the tattoo peeking out from under his shirt sleeve, to his eyebrow ring, to his overgrown hair—that he'd probably get tired of and shave completely off by week's end.

Ronnie was a lesson in contrasts. To me, he was funny, and could be one of the most charming people I knew. But he didn't extend the same courtesy to everyone. He had a limited supply of charm and couldn't afford to squander it. He said exactly what was on his mind, exactly when he wanted to say it, and it was so damn funny.

If somebody smelled bad, he'd greet them with: "Hey Stinky! You think deodorant's going on sale soon?" And, standing next to him, I was helpless to do anything but burst out laughing. I always told him he was taking me to Hell with him, just by association.

Yet, the very thing others found so unnerving about him, was the one thing that put me completely at ease. I knew exactly where I stood with Ronnie. If he was happy to see me, he smiled. If I said something funny, he laughed. And if I pissed him off, he yelled. There wasn't anything false about him.

"What are you staring at?" His terse question interrupted my reverie.

Embarrassed, I answered him in an accusing tone. "Nothing," then stood to throw away my paper plate.

"What is this shit we're listening to?" he asked as he gestured with his lighter to the overhead speakers. I mentally focused in on the music and answered, "'I Want a Man with a Slow Hand'… I love this song!"

"What the hell does that mean, 'A slow hand'?"

I looked at him, amused. "You know, in bed…" I waited a beat, "like you don't just rush to the big finish…"

He watched me across the table, with eyes squinted as he blew out a stream of smoke.

I waved him off. "Never mind. The fact that you *don't* know says it all."

He leaned forward and pulled the ashtray to him. "What? You got a problem with me being a hit 'em and quit 'em kind of guy?"

"No," I laughed. "I feel bad for Karen though."

"You let me worry about Karen."

A sharp rap sounded on the wall below. Our supervisor's way of signaling the end of lunchtime. We looked at each other for a split second, united in our irritation. Ronnie was the first to stand, while I shoved my lighter in my cigarette box.

"Let's go, Monie Baloney," he said.

I smiled. He had a nickname for every day of the week.

From: Amy
Sent: Wednesday, June 22, 2005 11:08 AM
To: Girls; Matt
Subject: Overheard in the Lunchroom

Preparing my lunch in the office kitchen today, I overheard one of our crack interns reading the instructions on her Smart Ones frozen meal:
*"What if it's just a **microwave**, and not a microwave **oven**??"*

I weep for the future.

Reply All
From: Mona

Okay...somebody has to say it...There goes the "you are what you eat" theory.

Reply All:
From: Bridget

God help us all.

Is she the daughter, cousin, niece, friend of a big wig?

Reply All
From: Amy

I hope she is. Summer is our most competitive season for interns. It would be a sad day if that kind of comment could come from someone who is supposed to be the cream-of-the-future-crop.

CHAPTER SIX

I ONCE HAD A COWORKER WHO I …well I can't say I hated him exactly, but what I felt for him was a volatile combination of anger and pity that I had never experienced before, and haven't experienced since. He was younger than me by a few years chronologically, but by light years in, what I thought was, maturity.

He had remained on friendly terms with Ryan, my son's absent father, long after Ryan had quit his job and left town—which might have explained my anger. He also loved a rousing game of Dungeons and Dragons, which was definitely where the pity came in. His name was Kevin. Life, up until that point, had never granted me a Kevin that I liked. Or a Vicki, but that's a different story.

Kevin was the kindest, most naïve person I had encountered since I was four years old, so of course I couldn't stand him. One of my coworkers and I would joke that he had a Sarcasm Meter that was out of gas. He just never picked up on any of the nastier social skills. Or maybe he did. Maybe he was exceedingly clever, and remained voluntarily ignorant of any negative behavior. But I wouldn't lay odds on that theory.

～

One morning, Kevin ran into a pallet of tuna with his forklift and some cans toppled to the floor.

"Oh for Christ's sake, Kevin!" I yelled, making it a much bigger deal than it needed to be.

"Sorry!" He apologized, in the lowest-on-the-food-chain way he had about him.

The cans were rolling around in my path, so I had to help him, and I did. But in the most unpleasant manner I could manage at 6:15 on a Tuesday morning. That was considerable since I had been up since five, and had already sharpened my skills on the Wonder Bread vendor, the produce truck driver, and our Dock Supervisor, Menzel. Calvin was his first name, but we never called him that. Just Menzel. "Menzel Washington," as Jason, another dock worker had termed him, and we had all picked up the habit.

"Now, Kevin, don't you let Pun'kin pick on you," warned Jim, the Pet Milk driver, as he rolled a milk rack out of his truck.

Jim winked at me as he passed by and I smiled. He was irresistible. He must have sensed how I felt about him, and that was why he called me "Pun'kin," when the other truck drivers called me something entirely different.

Jim always smelled like old milk, and the cold of his truck. He had one permanently crossed eye, and always claimed he had to drive ninety miles an hour down the highway because, "chicks dig Milk drivers."

"It's all the calcium," he would say. "Makes 'em horny."

Since Kevin didn't possess the foresight to park out of the way, it wasn't long until Ronnie came careening around the corner. Seeing Kevin's forklift in the way, he swore, jerked the brake, and drove his own lift hard to the right. Kevin jumped up to move his equipment, and I was left finishing his job in our now cramped quarters.

Unfortunately, Kevin's idea of getting out of Ronnie's way was to slowly reverse his forklift. Situated as we were, that meant one of the prongs of his forklift drifted slowly between my legs and scooped me up from behind as I bent over to pick up another can of tuna. I don't even want to think about the amount of damage he would have inflicted had space been anything but limited.

Alarmed, I shouted, "Hello! I'm losing my virginity, here!"

Jason, who had just joined the traffic jam and was lounging on his forklift nearby, hollered, "Hey! Watch your mouth Little Girl!" Jason always called me Little Girl because he was about ten feet tall, compared to my five feet, two inches.

Ronnie made a big show of looking around and added, "...there might be ladies present."

I looked up, "Oh. Sorry, Kev."

"Knock it off!" Menzel yelled, grabbing everybody's attention and cutting off any further conversation.

Menzel did a lot of yelling. I'd like to think it was to compensate for the constant noise level on the dock. The whine of forklifts, the rumble of a dock door opening, the roar of the bailer, and the constant phone ringing. But that wasn't it. No, Menzel did a lot of yelling because we were always making him mad.

He looked at me. "Find something to do, right now."

"Oh, I'm sorry, Menz," I started, rank with insincerity. "I'm a little busy being violated right now, but—" I heard Ronnie's grunt of laughter, and stopped talking to control my own, since Menzel looked less than amused.

"You two," he pointed at Ronnie and me, and pitched his voice over the boom and pop of the trash compactor. "Don't you start this bullshit again today!"

"Well, girls, this has been fun." Jim said, as he folded his paperwork and strolled off the dock.

Ronnie and I were indignant, but Menzel cut off our oncoming defenses with a round of commands. "Mona. Help Kevin with those cans."

I threw my hands up in frustration. "What the hell's it look like I'm doing—"

He ignored my outburst. "Ronnie! Take that milk out to the cooler. Jason, load up the bailer while you're waiting, and Kevin, get the hell out of the way!"

Kevin sprang into action, all rosy eagerness. "Okay!" He chirped.

"Call me!" I cried as he drove off the dock. Even Jason smiled at that, and he was rarely entertained by anything I did. When Menzel twisted around to glare at me, I held up my hands in defense.

"I'm done now. I swear."

Eventually, we all got back to work. Menzel left to bother Dawn in the Receiving Office. I finished unloading the beer truck. Then Ronnie and I unloaded a truck of four hundred and seventy tires. Jason ran freight over to the in-store Bakery. Kevin unloaded a few pallets of copy paper, and apologized about thirty-six more times that morning.

There are people who fall by the wayside in life. People you step on, insult, dismiss. Kevin was one of those people for me. By the time I met him, Life had kicked me straight in the chops a few too many times. I kicked back, but at the wrong times, the wrong people. I said things to him I wouldn't say to the devil himself.

Mean things. Spiteful things.

He never said a word to me that wasn't kind-hearted. He never yelled at me, never even tried to make me feel bad.

And do you know what I never did? I never thanked him.

I never thanked him for ignoring my spite.

I never thanked him for helping me whenever I asked for it.

And I never thanked him for the birthday gifts he had given my son every year since Will's father left town.

From: Bridget
Sent: Thursday July 14, 2005 10:09 AM
To: Girls, Matt
Subject: Fun Times at Work

We have someone in another office that is probably a long-lost relative to Amy's Microwave Oven co-worker. She sent out an email today, then at the end of the email she wrote out her email address so we could reply... (Hit reply???) Second, the email address she typed at the bottom was wrong. So I'm sitting here with my new favorite toy at work, it's called the Sarcastic Ball. (Cathy, if you were still here we would have worn the paint off it)

I ask it, "Will she ever learn?" The response- Yeah, and I'm the Pope.
Some of my other favorite responses: Who cares, Whatever, You've got to be kidding, Forget about it (I always add a Mob accent to this one)

Reply
From: Mona

I never knew the Sarcastic Ball existed. Why do I not have one?

Reply
From: Amy

Ditto. I NEED one. Just this morning I had a co-worker email to tell me his feelings were hurt by a joke I made. And it wasn't even that bad!! I'm so misunderstood.

Reply
From: Mona

Let me confirm: His feelings were hurt? Amy, you big bully.

Reply All
From: Bridget

I think he needs the Affirmation Ball.

Affirmation Ball Responses: At Least I Love You, Brilliant Idea!, Nice Outfit, Pure Genius!, Your Breath Is So Minty, You're 100% Fun!...

Reply All
From: Mona

Well, he needs some kind of ball, that's for sure.

Reply All
From: Amy

Stop it; I have to pee.

CHAPTER SEVEN

TOWARDS THE END OF MY TENURE at the "Hotel California"—which was what I called my job at the Warehouse because it felt like you could never leave—I began to truly hate most of the people who worked there. Not necessarily the people in my department. No, we were a tight group and had our share of fun. But I really began to resent people outside of my department, and their demands on my time.

I hated the guy in Hardlines who needed me to get a skid of motor oil out of the overhead steel because he couldn't drive a forklift. I hated the girl who ran her pallet jack into a load of cat food because that meant I had to restack the entire pallet, and those bags were fifty pounds a piece. And, I don't want to say I hated all managers in general, but certain ones weren't particularly bright.

So, when I was greeted one January morning by the dimmest bulb in the box and the command: "I need to talk to you!" I wasn't really surprised, or particularly impressed.

I dodged his pointed finger. "Can it wait 'til after break?"

"Yes!" He yelled again. *Moron.*

"Great! See you then!" I sent him a false smile as I crossed the room to the time clock.

My supervisor, who was standing behind me, started laughing quietly a moment later. There was no such thing as a united managerial front at that place.

"Whew! What'd you do now?"

"God only knows, Menz," I said. "God only knows."

Five minutes before break, I was paged to the office—lest I forget my important meeting. I headed to the front of the store, but I walked past the office, and into the break room. I made a cup of coffee, stirred in creamer, and grabbed two sugars. Finally, ten minutes after I was paged, I took a seat in the office. In short order, I found out I had insulted him and that I had an attitude problem— which wasn't really front-page news.

Whenever my supervisor's boss, Shane, called meetings, Ronnie would walk in the office and say, "Okay. What did Little Miss do now?" Little Miss being short for "Little Miss Can't-Be-Wrong," a song that frequently played over the store's speaker system.

And then Shane would join in the hilarity. He'd pick up a pad of paper and pretend to check off items as he said,

"Mona needs to be nicer to Katie.

"Mona needs to be nicer to Darryl.

"Mona needs to be nicer to Jean.

"Mona needs to be nicer to…" Ha ha ha. Just a laugh a minute, they were.

This particular manager had just recently been dumped by Lynn, which was unfortunate. And by unfortunate, I mean for me. It was patently obvious that, since Lynn had quit before they began dating, and therefore was not around, he just wanted to take his anger out on anyone who gave him half a reason.

I'm sure it helped that I was close to Lynn. And that, yes, I had insulted him. But it was mainly a personal grudge, and once I realized that, I stared at his mottled face and refused to respond.

Well, okay, I didn't. I wish I could have. I wanted to. But I just can't be yelled at without returning the favor. His biggest grievance was that I had insulted him behind his back. I apologized for that, and then insulted him to his face, which—believe me—didn't help.

When his final tirade was over, I asked, "You finished?"

"Yes!" he shot.

"Good." I stood up. "I got another truck to unload. I don't have time to talk to you all day."

That sparked another round of shouting which was, quite possibly, the funniest thing I had ever completely ignored. I put on my weight belt, stuffed my box knife into one of the back pockets of my jeans, then turned on my walkie-talkie and clipped it onto the other. I picked up my coffee and opened the office door.

And in—what I assumed was—a last ditch effort to find a dig that would finally hurt me, he said, "You want to be a teacher right?"

I stopped in the open doorway, but didn't turn to face him. "Yes."

He gave a low, self-important laugh. "Good luck," he said. "Nobody's gonna give a shit about you and your attitude."

Without a word, I walked out of the office. As I rounded the corner, Ronnie fell in step beside me. His presence brought me up short.

"What are you doing here?"

He shrugged. "Just came to see how it was going..."

We turned and headed back to the dock together. After we had passed the bakery and the produce department, I slanted a questioning glance at him.

"You hear everything?"

He gave a short nod. "Yep."

Once back in our department, Ronnie grabbed the paperwork hanging on the clipboard for dock door Three, which left me the Procter and Gamble load in door Five. "Bastard," I muttered, then snatched the paperwork from the board.

Ronnie stepped onto his forklift, his short laugh drowned by the sound of a passing flatbed. He started to drive away, but stopped, almost immediately.

"Hey, Mona," he said.

I looked up from my study of the P&G paperwork to see a ghost of a smile pass over his face.

He jerked his chin toward the front of the store. "I thought you were awesome up there."

I stared after him as he drove away. Ronnie made me feel disoriented every so often. As if I was seeing something out of the corner of my eye, but if I tried to look directly at it, it was gone. While most of the time he didn't appear to pay me any particular notice, every now and then, I got the impression he did. But, I had learned along the way that his moods were impossible to understand or predict, so I no longer even tried.

I knocked on the plexi-glass window of the Receiving Office. Dawn looked up, and I waved my paperwork so she could see it.

"Ready?" she asked, the question muffled through the window.

I nodded. "Send him in."

The sound of a buzzer filled the air, as the door from the waiting room opened. Without looking at the driver, I said, "Follow me," and led him back to open his trailer door.

It's funny how time can change your perspective. While at that time, I thought I knew what love looked like, I now know that I never recognized it. As the years pass, I have often wondered if it is possible to want someone a little, to love someone just a little. And, if so, what is it that tips the scales? What sends us into a love affair with one person, but only friendship with another? Is it passion?

Chemistry? Or is it really something as little as one person making the first move? Can it be possible for a great love of your life to slip through your fingers because of something as arbitrary as poor timing?

I sometimes wonder what would have become of our friendship had Ronnie and I worked together longer. But, I also know that, at the time, I never would have dated someone who played paintball in his spare time and was pierced in more places than I was. It was too far outside my little world. And I imagine my life, filled with trips to the zoo and Sesame Street, was a little crowded for him as well. As it was, after working together closely for almost four years, Ronnie left three weeks after I became engaged to a guy named John, and I've never seen him since.

From: Mona
Sent: Monday, June 27, 2005 11:41 AM
To: Girls
Subject:

Will has decided he wants to be a clown. This is a
transformation that will take-by his estimate-three days. He
does not care that I hate clowns, and he assures me he will
not be a scary one. For his "clown kit," he has a piece of red
material wrapped in tape (for his clown nose, I presume),
a deck of cards that he holds behind his back and fans with
his fingers to produce "gas." He has a basket for his head that
makes him look like a Shriner, and a water bottle that he
sprayed me with twice "on accident" before I wrestled it away
from him.

Reply
From: Christian

Sounds like a normal day at my house.

Reply
From: Mona

Now he's in the garage teaching himself to juggle with oranges.
All I can hear are the sounds of thumping and frustration.

Reply
From: Stagner

At least he's in the garage. My boys practice juggling in the
family room.

CHAPTER EIGHT

ONE EVENING THIS PAST WINTER, OUR family was gathered together watching television. Soon, my husband Dan left the room to get a bowl of ice cream. Will and I stayed as we were. Absorbed in the commercials. When a commercial came on for…diapers, I suppose—something that required lots of squealing children—Will said:

"I hate that kid there who hogs all the attention."

And my immediate response was this:

"Oh I don't know if we need to hate kids on the TV screen do we?"

Which wasn't half bad, until I added, "Not when there are so many people in real life we can hate." And the sad truth was that he seemed to think I had a very good point. If this is my parenting style, should I be reproducing? I have wondered often.

My guilt over the life I gave my son in his early years keeps me awake some nights. And has become, from time to time, crippling in its intensity. When I became a mother for the first time, I was barely twenty-one. I was not in a happy place in my life and I couldn't distance myself enough to gain any real perspective. Will's biological father and I had split up when he was three months old and by the time he was nine months, the Father of the Year had moved back to the greener pastures of his hometown and started yet another family. This I have heard third and fourth-hand, as I never saw him again after he left.

Child support was non-existent, which was fine, I'm no martyr. I wanted him gone and he left. But being without him left a financial hole in my life that found me on welfare and in subsidized housing. I swore to myself that I'd only be on the taxpayers' nickel for one year. And I kept that promise.

In the meantime I worked forty hours a week to make ends meet, and since my parents were living in Chicago at the time, my grandparents watched Will one night a week so I could attend night school. After paying the leftover hospital bills, rent, utilities, childcare, and an unhealthy amount of monthly credit card debt, I had not a whole lot of money left. I scraped together enough to buy Will his food. Ramen noodles became the main staple of my diet. Well, and cigarettes. I told you I was no martyr.

It went on this way for some time. And while I loved my son so much it hurt, it also scared me, this love for another person. It made me slightly wary of becoming too close to him, and that left me ignorant of his tender needs.

To solve a mutual money shortage, my boyfriend, John, and I moved in together, and eventually married. The romance of it all fairly blows me away—even now. It was easy for us to get along, though. We were both funny, witty, and equally cynical. But it didn't work. Like the proverbial oil and water, you could put us in the same place, shake us up, and we'd mix well, but never really become *one*.

Then, one day—my 25th birthday—I couldn't take it anymore. I told John that I didn't feel like he had any relationship with Will. Didn't even particularly like him. It surprised me that he answered honestly.

"You know…I just don't."

God love honesty, even if it does slice you in two.

To be fair, our marriage had been over long before that night. His words simply sealed its fate sooner rather than later. Whether he meant he didn't feel he had a relationship with Will, or he actually didn't like him, I never asked. It didn't matter. Either way, I had no choice but to leave.

So, after living together for two full years, I wanted a divorce after only nine months of marriage. I recognize that John didn't deserve the treatment he got from me in the end; all the confusion and the anger that came out of nowhere. But if all life is a balance and you get what you give, then he did deserve it slightly. He alternated between ignoring my son and making him feel like an idiot; yet he had his own daughter who he loved as much as any child deserves. The difference in his treatment of the two children was both obvious and pathetic.

We met at our house one night a few weeks later to take stock of our joint belongings and such. We had every square inch of the dining room table covered with checkbooks, bills, bank statements, and mortgage papers.

He said to me, "Look at all this," and motioned to the overly laden table. "Do you hate me this much?"

I glanced at the table. I thought about everything that had to be done and undone. "Yes I do." But I hated myself more.

The day I had to leave our house stands as one of the worst in my memory. Divorce, for any reason, is devastating in a way that cannot be conveyed. It is a pervasive sadness that you cannot hide from, yet cannot face. It was so much deeper and bleaker than I had imagined as a child, when I dreamed of becoming a statistic.

For me, it was the little things that became unbearable: the toothbrush holder with only one toothbrush, the windows stripped of their curtains, the empty cabinets in the kitchen. Even though I knew it was the right thing to do, I will never forget the hopelessness of my last day, in that lonely house.

My car was in the shop, so my mom came over to collect my last few things, and then drive me home to her house. Away from a place I no longer wanted to be, but was unbelievably reluctant to leave. When she took the last box out to the car, I did a final check of the rooms. Picking up a penny here. A Lego there.

Mom came back in, and I was standing at the kitchen window, so weighed down with everything I had done and lost that I couldn't move. Could barely breathe. She didn't touch me. Maybe she sensed that I couldn't have borne it. Instead, she walked silently to my side and stood there. Together, we looked out over the backyard. Mrs. Sayers, the next door neighbor, was trimming back her rampant honeysuckle vine. The boy who lived on the other side of us was playing ball with a stray dog he had found that no one had ever claimed.

Not since I was a child had I had neighbors I actually knew. That I talked to over the fence on Saturday afternoons. That I sat on the porch with in the evenings after work. For some reason, it was the loss of my neighbors that got to me the most.

Mom must have seen me bow my head, because she turned to me and cleared her throat. "I've been where you are…and if I could take this from you, I would."

I didn't respond, and I doubt she expected me to.

Then she rested her hand on top of mine. "I'll be in the car. Stay here as long as you need to." She pushed off the counter with her hip, and walked away—her fading footsteps echoing in the empty room. My mom is not a woman often blessed with the right words in times of trial. She yells when silence is called for, cries when we need her to be strong. Still, no matter what has passed or the future holds, on that day, she was perfect.

As the screen door slammed behind her, I dashed impatiently at the tears rolling down my face. Uncomfortable, as always, with vulnerability. I wanted to ignore any messy emotions. I couldn't afford a crack in my façade. But at that point, the pain was unstoppable and I leaned on the counter and let it overwhelm me.

Back then, I had a nasty habit of staying in relationships until something better came down the pike. That may sound heartless to you, but hey, the truth isn't always pretty. So, I guess this relationship ended the same way all of my relationships ended.

I finally realized there was another guy I liked better.

He was about three feet tall, he was four years old, and he was better off with no father figure at all, than one who cared so little.

From: Amy
Sent: Tuesday, April 12, 2005 11:42 AM
To: Mona
Subject: Some people call me Maurice.

Who is Maurice Chevalier? He must have been somebody.
His words grace the top of my calendar for today:

"My own experience has taught me this: if you wait for the
perfect moment, when all is safe and assured, it may never
arrive."

That's my theory on driving.

Reply
From: Mona

I'm pretty sure he was an actor or a singer a while ago. People
always ask me if I'm related to him- well they don't any more.

Reply
From: Amy

Now do they now ask you if you're related to the doctor who
treated John Wilkes Booth?

Chapter Nine

I FIRST MET MY EX-HUSBAND, JOHN, while working at the Wholesale Club. I had known him for while, but never really noticed him until he switched from working overnights, to working daytime hours. I liked him. He was always funny, and he had a daughter, so I didn't have to worry that he would be uncomfortable with my single parent status.

After we had been dating for about a year, he quit, and found a different job. He was fondly remembered by my colleagues—much more beloved than me—so the fact that I eventually divorced him presented a bit of a problem.

My immediate co-workers were among the few I actually admired. Although I could tell they couldn't understand why I was divorcing him, they still provided their silent support—thereby demonstrating why I respected them in the first place.

John's sister was a manager that I had always considered a friend. She was the only one who could have justifiably made my job difficult. Yet, she was classy enough to avoid that. Mainly by avoiding me, but who am I to split hairs? And while the loss of her friendship was hurtful, it was no less than I expected, or deserved.

Of course, there were those who felt the need to openly question my actions—but not to me directly. Rather, they discussed it amongst themselves, and drew their own inane conclusions. They took it upon themselves to make veiled comments while I was on break, and call me names under their breath when I walked past them.

I'd like to say it hurt my feelings, because that would make me a more sympathetic character. But it would also make me a liar. It simply irritated me, and in a perverse way, it amused me. This idea that the people going out of their way to cast stones at me were the exact same people who I wouldn't have crossed the street to talk to in the first place.

What I never bothered to explain to them was that John wasn't a bad guy, and I never said he was. He loved his daughter. He could be very charming. And, to this day, he still holds the record for some of the funniest comments my girlfriends and I have ever heard. But our marriage was divided from the very beginning. It was divided by the wall he had erected between himself and the rest of the world. It was also crowded with his pride, and his overdeveloped sense of duty towards certain people in his life. There was no room for me, and definitely no room for my son.

And what they never would have understood was that I had finally realized it was okay to be different. That although others before me may have found it necessary to accept those aspects of his personality, I didn't. And although many of the women around me were willing to settle for a relationship in which their emotional needs weren't being met, I wasn't.

While divorce proceedings were underway, I had the bad taste to remark that a member of the construction crew—currently working in our store—was cute. So, my noble break-up was tarnished by the infidelity rumors I had to dodge at the end of it. As if anyone ever divorced their spouse and uprooted their child simply because someone different was easy on the eyes. But, I swear, that was the quality of intellect I was dealing with.

I defended myself to John alone, as he was the only one who deserved a response to that particular bit if lunacy. He might have believed me, and he may not have. But it was the truth, so I hope he did.

About two months after John and I separated, I quit my job and found a different one, working in a school. I doubled up on college classes, moved in with my parents, and finished my degree in education.

The friends I had made while working there, I haven't seen in years. But sometimes I wake up in the morning with a peculiar feeling, and I know I must have dreamt of them. I wake up missing them, and the sadness momentarily overcomes me. But I can't go back, and I won't. Sometimes it's just better to leave everything behind.

As for the rest of them—all of those people who had so much to say—I never knew what it was they collectively decided about me. I know they had to decide something, if only to have their own lives make sense. Maybe I had a nervous breakdown? Maybe I was crazy? Maybe I am. But I just couldn't be there anymore. That life. That job. That marriage. They were suffocating to me.

And just because I could, I asked that construction guy out on a date, and he said yes. We had a strange little dinner. No dessert. But he was a gentlemen and I was a mess. I'm sure that place erupted with rumors after our date. By then, I had already started my new life, so I never had to deal with them. Besides, as my friend Dawn always said—

Well…you know what they say about people who can't take a joke.

PART THREE:
FRIENDSHIP

"...that is the best—to laugh with someone because you both think the same things are funny."

~Gloria Vanderbilt, b.1924
American designer

From: Mona
Sent: Monday, June 14, 2003 1:24 PM
To: Girls
Subject: Girls Weekend

Okay I'm feeling a little bit out of the loop. Normally I would have received an invoice by now detailing all of the money I need to cough up for girl's weekend, or at the very least an itinerary of meeting places and times. Yes, I admit that I laugh a bit at this. I admit that I have, from time to time, rolled my eyes at the ceaseless flurry of emails regarding our trip. But I will now apologize for that since I know the alternative is to receive NO INFORMATION WHATSOEVER. What the hell is going on? Is anybody out there? Hello? Hello? Are we still going? I feel like any minute now I'll have to (gasp!) develop some plan of my own.

Reply All
From: Bridget

I second that! Amy's slacking these days.

Reply All
From: Amy

Ahem. Slacker my ass. You all know how to work your computers too.

Reply All
From: Mona

I found a swimsuit, though. It fits. I can't actually claim it's cute, but thank God it's red, white and blue. That'll show those terrorists.

Reply All
From: Cathy

I'm just wearing a sack. I think I've got back fat.

Reply All
From: Megan

OK. That made me laugh out loud and my students are reading.

CHAPTER TEN

EVERY SUMMER THE GIRLS AND I take a weekend trip down to a place called the Lake of the Ozarks in Missouri. It gives us a chance to get together, get away, and catch up with each other. We stay in Amy's family's condo which is situated on the water, and has a swimming pool nearby for the condo residents and their guests.

Normally we come down in shifts on Friday afternoon. The first wave—which is Bridget, Lynn and me—is responsible for the food, water and sport drinks, as well as airing out the condo, and wiping down the patio chairs. We used to be in charge of rafts, cool cups, and water noodles too, but now we just leave them down there.

The second wave (which is only Cathy) is responsible for the beer. An odd occurrence, since she's the only one who lives in Arkansas— and a dry county in Arkansas, at that. We'd change it, but she doesn't seem to mind stopping off at a liquor store just past the Missouri State line. Says she needs to get a Dr. Pepper, anyway.

The third wave, which is usually the rest of them, is only responsible for their own belongings. And they need to bring us each a beer when they come outside and join us in the pool. Girl's Weekend—for the most part—follows the same pattern every year.

It isn't a schedule we've consciously devised, or agreed to in an even remotely organized fashion. It's just that nobody seems to have a problem with it, so we stick with what works.

One particular year, it was only Cathy, Megan, Amy, Bridget, and me. We five were usually joined by three more, but it was a slow year. Christian was visiting her family in Maryland, and Stagner was the godmother at her nephew's baptism. Lynn was pregnant so she didn't feel like going, and although we always try to get Matt to go as well, he never joins us at Girls Weekend. He says he's not *that* gay.

We came down on Friday, as always, but in one single wave that threw things slightly off balance. By Saturday morning, we were back on an even keel. We rented a boat and headed to a secluded cove. We spent all of the long afternoon alternately swimming, lazing on the boat, and relaxing on our rafts in the water. We greeted the few passers-by we saw, but were wholly content to remain in the world of our own making. Talking to each other about a lot of nothing, and little bit of everything.

Late in the afternoon, we dragged our sore, sun-baked bodies back to the condo and prepared for the evening ahead. Saturday nights were reserved for going out to dinner and hitting the bars. In the early morning hours, we finally returned to the condo and fell into an exhausted and giddy slumber. And by Sunday afternoon, we were on our way home—without ever having indulged in a naked pillow fight—as some men we know would, perhaps, suggest.

The car was silent except for the occasional muted comment, and the sound of Cathy flipping the pages of a magazine. Megan was staring out the window, Amy was resting her eyes, and Bridget was looking through my CD collection.

We were driving along a lonely stretch of Highway 54 in central Missouri when I said to no one in particular:

"Gretchen."

Bridget looked at me from the passenger seat. "Who?"

"Gretchen." I repeated.

She flipped a glance out her window. "What?" Then back to me. "What are you talking about?"

"We just drove through Fulton, Missouri. Whenever I drive through different towns, I try to think about what types of people live there."

"And you think there's a Gretchen who lives in Fulton?"

"Yes." Then I caught her dubious expression. "I'm serious, Bridge—"

She laughed in reply. "Oh, I'm sure you are… that's the scary part."

"No, really, she's about twenty-eight years old now. She was the best looking girl in her high school class, but she really wasn't all that pretty."

"Poor Gretchen…"

I shrugged. "Yeah…her hair is too long, though." I gave the matter more thought. "She keeps it that way because she thinks her husband likes it…and she's right, he does…but it has lots of split ends, and about an inch and a half of her roots are showing."

Bridget laughed then, in the way she always does, like she's been taken by surprise, and can't believe she's actually amused.

"What are you guys talking about?" Amy shouted from the backseat. She can't ever be left in the dark. Curiosity may have killed the cat, but it never got Amy.

Bridget threw an answer over her shoulder, "You don't want to know."

"Yes I do. Hey! Stop at that Taco Bell."

As I pulled off the highway, Bridget told Amy, Megan and Cathy all about Gretchen from "Fenton" which is another town entirely, but she's always wrecking something – a cliché, a song lyric, or in this case, an entire town.

After hearing the story Amy caught my eye in the rearview mirror. "There's just something off about you…" she concluded.

Megan continued to stare out the window and said, "Exactly…" Which is what she always says when she's not listening or just doesn't feel like forming a response.

Cathy, who wasn't even pretending to listen, slapped her magazine on the console, effectively ending our conversation. "Look at this chick in this picture," she said. "God! She is so *ugly*."

Bridget recoiled. "Geez…" was all she said.

"How can you be *that* rich and *that* ugly?"

"Oh Cat, she is not ugly," Amy argued. "She's just different looking."

Cathy was unconvinced. "Yeah. Different from pretty."

From: Mona
Sent: Monday January 03, 2005 9:25 AM
To: Girls, Matt
Subject: tsunami

We are running a (not even close) second to Japan in the amount of money we have given to the tsunami relief effort, and we just came on TV claiming to be heading the "largest relief effort in the world". Is it necessary that we claim to be number one even when we, clearly, are not? No wonder people hate us.

Reply
From: Matt

Mona, we are the US of freaking A. We will not be bothered by technicalities—especially when it comes to the Japs. I'm sure somehow the numbers have been doctored and we really are #1. I am also sure that 74% of our countrymen cannot pronounce tsunami correctly.

Reply
From: Mona

My dear departed grandpa would agree wholeheartedly with you, as he hated the Japs. Something about Pearl Harbor really stuck with him. And, after all, it is so important to hold an entire race responsible for the actions of one generation.

CHAPTER ELEVEN

MY FRIEND MATT IS GAY. I don't announce that as if it's his defining characteristic, but rather so you get a feel for why he's always hanging out with a bunch of girls. Besides, if Matt has a defining characteristic, it's his sense of humor. There have been occasions when I have begged him to stop telling a story—if only for a minute—for fear that I had strained some vital organ.

I've known Matt was gay since my husband, Dan, pointed it out to me. We were standing in the kitchen getting ready for the evening ahead. Dan was staying home with the kids and I was going out with the girls. And Matt. Dan had just slid a pizza in the oven when he asked, "Who's going tonight?"

"Oh, you know, Amy, Lynn, Cathy and all them. And Matt... Ooh! A Christmas card from Aunt Mary!"

Dan turned to grab the Christmas card. I opened the credit card statement, cringed, and slid it back under the pile of mail.

"Matt? I thought she was dating a guy named John?"

"She is. This is her friend Matt."

"Oh..." He said, as he turned his attention to Will. "Hey! Turn that down!" Then back to me. "How does John feel about that?"

"I don't know and I don't think Cathy ever asked."

"Are they really friends? Or are they, you know, *friends*?" He asked with a suggestive wiggle of his eyebrows. I rolled my eyes. This is the man I've chosen to spend the rest of my life with. I held out a magazine to Dan who was now standing across the kitchen island from me.

"Here. Another one of those Cabelas catalogues…"

"Oh cool!" He made a grab for it. But I pulled it just out of his reach and looked up at him. "And no, they are not *friends*," I imitated his earlier expression, "as you put it…"

I took the pile of mail and started toward the office. But I stopped, surprised, when Dan asked yet another question. Dan's not a real chatty guy, so it always catches me off-guard when he's chock full of conversation.

"We're talking about Cathy right?"

I put the mail down and gave him my full attention. "Yes."

"Good-looking Cathy?"

"Yes." I snapped. "Good Looking Cathy."

"Have they ever slept together?"

"No, they're just friends, have been since middle school."

Dan laughed in disbelief and leaned into our conversation. "Cathy has been friends with Matt since middle school and he's never once tried to sleep with her?"

I shook my head. Dan slammed both hands on the kitchen island and announced, "He's gay."

"No, Dan…"

"Gay!" He yelled over my protest.

94

"He is not! They're just friends!"

He opened the refrigerator and looked back at me. "Uh...and he's gay," he said, then cracked open a beer. I guess so I wouldn't go confusing Matt's sexual preference with his own.

As I watched Dan swallow his beer whole, I thought about it. "I think he likes women..." But my mind was racing to find any mention of a past girlfriend, or any woman period.

"Maybe he's bisexual." Dan suggested. "Although if that was the case, he'd still want to sleep with Cathy."

I dismissed that with a wave. "There's no such thing. 'Bisexual is just the last stop on the train to Gaytown.'"

Dan laughed. "You make that up?"

"I don't think so. I think I heard it somewhere."

"Probably read it ..."

"Maybe. I can't imagine I'm that clever."

Well into the evening, the idea stuck with me. Was he gay? It wasn't something I had ever been faced with on a personal level. For about two minutes, I really thought hard about it. And then I remembered that I couldn't possibly care less. And no matter what, this I know: if Matt ever had someone, I would welcome that person completely.

It was sometime later while watching news about a high profile criminal trial that Matt felt he needed to out himself. He found it alarming—this idea that a person would have such secrets hidden from their loved ones. It struck a nerve with him and he didn't want to be one of those people who lead secret lives. So he asked Cathy if he could come over one night and have a talk with her.

It was unnerving to her, all his secrecy. What did he want? What was he going to say? We all told her he was going to break his gay news to her, but she refused that theory. He's just asexual, she would say.

When he finally broke the news, Cathy was relieved.

"Well, thank God!" She responded. "I thought you were going to tell me you were in love with me."

So now, around the holidays we all get together and somebody asks Matt when he's going to tell his parents. This year the place was Casa Gallardo Restaurant, and it was my turn.

"Jack on *Will and Grace* says you should always come out at the holidays, and Christmas is just around the corner."

He corrected me. "No. I saw that episode. Lesbians come out at Christmas; gay men come out at Thanksgiving."

I picked at my nachos. "Well, thank God you've got a whole 'nother year!"

"Yeah...and I'm waiting for my parents to do something really traumatic so I can blame it on *that*."

"Matt!" Cathy interrupted. "For God's sake! Your mom and sister take you shopping when they need to pick out curtains...I'm pretty sure they know."

I looked at Matt and nodded. "They know."

Lynn looked around the table, "I don't know...do you think they *really* know for sure, though?" She's always good for that little kernel of doubt.

"Curtains?" Bridget dipped her chip in the salsa. "They totally know."

"You're right." Matt decided. "I'm doing it. 'Mom. Dad. I'm gay. Could you please pass the turkey?'"

We all laughed. He sat back in his chair, and signaled the waitress for another drink. "I'm pretty sure that's how I'm going to break the news..."

From: Mona
Sent: Wednesday, April 13, 2005 10:12AM
To: Cathy
Subject: Mud on the Tires

Do you think my last name guarantees me a ticket to Brad Paisley's Muddstock '05 Concert?

Reply
From: Cathy

I hate the video for that song - I wouldn't go if I thought crazy kids were going to be throwing mud around—and that's not because I'm old—I wouldn't have gone when I was their age. Haven't you ever played mud volleyball- mud in places I'd rather not think of...

Reply
From: Mona

I've never played mud volleyball- never even heard of it- but I was on a sand volleyball team once. It carries the same type of "foreign substance in every crevice" thing that leads me to believe I would not actually enjoy an afternoon in the mud either. And while I have to wonder if Muddstock is an actual event, or simply one fabricated for a music video, I do love that Brad Paisley.

Reply
From: Cathy

I know you love him—and that scares me a little—he is so tiny...and his cowboy hat is so big on his teeny little head.

Reply
From: Mona

*Need I remind you that Matt Damon isn't exactly an
Amazon?*

Reply
From: Cathy

*Yes, well that is true, but I've never seen Brad Paisley scale
a building while carrying a knack sack full of fake passports
and foreign currency, have I?*

Chapter Twelve

IF ANYONE WATCHES ME CLOSELY IN public long enough, they will surely see me bow my head and smile to myself every so often. Then I'll search frantically for a gum wrapper, a receipt—any scrap of paper—and after finding it, scribble something down and throw it in my purse.

I go on about my day, repeating this pattern every so often at red lights, in the checkout lane or before pulling out of the parking lot. Much later in the day, or perhaps the next, I will find these scraps of paper and sit down at the keyboard. Because when I smiled, I was watching you, or listening to you, and without knowing it, you sparked a story in my mind.

At other times, the tales I spin have no other source but my imagination. I like to imagine the fun I could have making a gigantic scene in public. I get a kick out of picturing the expressions on people's faces.

Behind a slow person in the grocery aisle, I imagine yelling, "Move! I'm in labor!"

While it's obvious to the onlookers that I am not nine months pregnant, or even one month for that matter, I'd start knocking bottles of water off the shelves and continue shouting as they bounce and splash.

"My water just broke! For the love of God, somebody call an ambulance!"

Really, what would people do? They can't ignore me, I'm too weird. But they can't look at me either, because to take part in my strange, one-act play would be a real drain on their time.

I also like to envision the fall-out from an inappropriate comment, or an ill-timed question. Cathy and Matt are my favorite people to play this game with, as they are more than willing to indulge my imagination, and I theirs. And it's especially fun to contemplate on vacation, when there's a very slim chance you will ever see these people again.

When Cathy and I visited the town of Savannah this past spring, we wore out our shoes touring every historical home to be found within walking distance. We were especially excited about the Mercer House of "Midnight in the Garden of Good and Evil" fame.

Let me save you some time, and caution you not to mention the movie, should you find yourself in Savannah. The folks there were not as impressed by the movie as they were by the book. However, if you want to be immediately shunned, go ahead and mention it.

You may remember that Jim Mercer—the main character in the book—was as renowned for his art collection and lavish parties as he was for his unconventional relationships. In the parlor of the Mercer House, there is a custom made chair. I cannot remember the name of it, but what appears to be the back of the chair forms the shape of a "C," and is actually the front of the chair. Gentlemen straddled it, so their coat tails could hang down their back without gathering up and wrinkling.

On the tour I digested that information without a blink. But afterwards, as we sat in one of Savannah's many Squares, I did wish for a different ending to that tour.

I said to Cathy, "I wish I'd have had the nerve to say, 'Listen, Ma'am, why don't you cut the crap and tell us what that chair is really used for,' then wink at her, real obnoxious-like."

Then Cathy, knowing her cue, jumped in. "As I lean over to that big, black security guard and go, 'Lady Chablis? Is it really you?"

I laughed and Cathy went on. "Or since they never want us to talk about the movie, what if I had just walked right into the library and laid face-down on the rug, like Jude Law when he died in that scene—"

"—as I throw myself violently into the bookcase, and pretend to have heart failure..." I added.

We laugh at our cleverness, as if we would ever say or do those kinds of things in our entire lives. Unfortunately, we've been raised to well. We just follow along with the tour, smiling, nodding, and being respectful of the dead as well as the living. When we're finished, we look the tour guides in the eye, thank them, and quietly shut the door behind us. It's just the idea that is tantalizing. The idea of escaping so far from your own personality—if only for a moment—that just seems irresistible.

To be perfectly honest, from the moment we arrived until the second we left, it was apparent why the people of Savannah are known for their hospitality. We had a wonderful time, and would like to thank the following people:

1. During our tour of the Owens-Thomas House (built around 1819), a woman in a sleeveless Harley Davidson shirt pointed to the ramp on the second floor and said to the tour guide—who somehow managed not to laugh—"That must be for wheelchair access."

   Yes, handicap accessibility was a big architectural movement in the early 19th century.

   Oh, the fun we had with that.

   "Do you think these smoke alarms are original to the house?" We'd whisper to each other.

   "How about that plastic hose reel? It looks really old."

2. Thank you to every trolley driver, cashier, and tour guide in the city. Every one of them asked us for our student I.D., even though I'm thirty-one and Cathy is thirty-two. We appreciate it.

3. Thank you to the southern gentleman who ran our tour of one of the houses near Madison Square in historic Savannah.

We don't know his name, although we still affectionately refer to him as "Mr. M"—in deference to the fake diamond *M* on the lens of his sunglasses. We loved how he would bang his cane on the floor to move the along the stragglers during the tour. *Bang! Bang! Bang!* "We're ready!" He would yell.

And we loved how, upon hearing Cathy was from Arkansas, he looked down his nose at her, with a vague air of distaste. "Oh..." he muttered in a perfectly lazy southern drawl. "I didn't know anybody was *from* Arkansas..."

4. Late Saturday night, after a trip to the Seafood Festival along the Savannah River, Cathy and I walked back to our hotel. The walk began with a hellacious set of steps: curved from much use, steep and numerous. I was about five steps from the top, pleading with Jesus and every saint I could think of, and calling instructions over my shoulder.

    "Don't be a hero Cath! Grab on to the railing!" (And before you go passing judgment, they were just as hard to climb sober.) When a woman passed us, beginning her descent, I looked at her and said, "I must be getting old." She said, "Oh honey, don't you worry about it, everybody calls on Jesus when they walk up these steps." Of course I loved her instantly.

5. And finally, thank you to every man who dons a loose tank top or sports a fanny pack in public. Thank you especially to the man who crossed our path wearing both. It prompted Cathy to say, once he was out of earshot,

"Sir. I don't know what it is, but the combination of your fanny pack and your blousy tank top is completely erotic to me."

Which prompted me to laugh so hard that I almost got hit by a trolley.

From: Aunt Lou
Sent: Tuesday, May 03, 2005 5:25 PM
To: Ramona
Subject: Carrie

Ramona, your cousin Carrie will be visiting from L.A. from June 17-20. I'm having everyone over during that time. Your mom and I have tickets for Man of La Mancha at Stages on the 19th.

Reply All
From: Mona

Stages? Didn't that used to be a bar and dance club? I'd be concerned about which version of Man of La Mancha you're going to see.

Reply
From: Aunt Lou

Ramona, your mother has been to the theater in many cities and, indeed, countries but she will tell you that Man of La Mancha is the greatest thing since life's bread.

Reply
From: Mona

I will be making fun of you for the rest of my life. It's "The greatest thing since SLICED bread."

Reply
From: Aunt Lou

*When your mother and I were kids, and someone said
something that didn't seem quite real we said, "Like Fish."
Who knows what that means. When I met your Uncle Tom
(some 30 years ago) I said something that wasn't quite true
and he said, "White Fish." We had an uppercrust/lowercrust
argument as to who was right, and lo and behold, we couldn't
come to a conclusion.*

*Which brings me to your rebuttal. "The greatest thing since
life's bread" I think that could mean that bread is the staff of
life. "The greatest thing since sliced bread" makes it necessary
to know when bread started to be sliced, and who actually
knows that? I think this is a draw. Have a great Mother's Day
in Savannah. We will be thinking of you while we're here.*

Reply
From: Mona

*I think it is, in fact, NOT a draw and you are making all of
that up. Life's bread? I never realized bread was the staff of
life- perhaps you mean "stuff." Even so, I say to you, "White
fish" because your suppositions don't seem quite real to me.*

*Anyway, I hope everyone's Mother's Day goes well. I will be
thinking of you all as well and I tour the Old South and sleep
with mosquitoes as big as my head. Ta!*

CHAPTER THIRTEEN

WHEN CATHY AND I TOOK A trip to Savannah this spring, we were going in blind. Neither of us had ever been there, which isn't all that surprising in my case, I have two small children. Travel ranks pretty low on my life's list of perks.

It did surprise me that Cathy had never been there, though. For two reasons. One, she is very well-traveled. I think that because she's been to Ireland and, to me, if you've visited somewhere in Europe, it doesn't matter if you've been anywhere else. Secondly, Cathy loves the history of the Old South, so cities in that region of the country are a common destination for her. She often threatens to abduct tour guides or Civil War re-enactors, tie them to a chair in her apartment, and force them to recite historical facts while she takes a bubble bath.

"Tell me more about the Confederates…" she'd say.

My point is that Cathy travels more than I do. In light of this fact, she booked my flight, and reserved our hotel room. Since she was already in Georgia on business, she also picked me up from the airport, because I am completely helpless when I'm allowed to be.

All I was required to do was make it—somehow unassisted—through my layover in Atlanta which, thankfully, I did without any major upheaval. I'm always a little bit anxious that my desire to make a scene is going to finally assert itself in the airport, so being there makes me a little twitchy.

Being in Atlanta's airport was especially nerve-wracking because I once had a very bad date with a guy from Atlanta. I worried that Fate would find it necessary for us to meet again, so in an effort to avoid that, I spent a substantial portion of my time behind postcard racks or walking quickly and along the wall. Not that I was in any danger of him seeing me and striking up the band either, I just didn't want to run smack into him without any preparation.

It made me feel sorry for famous people. I was trying to avoid one person who wouldn't be able to pick me out of a police line-up, and these poor people have to hide in plain sight from an entire population. And then they're expected to be friendly. Yikes. No, I'll take unfriendly and anonymous any day of the week.

But all in all I love the airport—or any major transportation hub, for that matter—for the people-watching I can do. But it presents its own set of problems. First of all, I don't like to talk to people I don't know. Oh, sure, I smile. I say hello. I live in the Midwest. Custom dictates that I'm naturally friendly, but it needs to stop there. I have friends. I have no immediate need to find a new one in a cab.

To combat the overly friendly and the friendless, I carry a magazine when I travel. There are a couple of reasons for choosing a magazine over a book.

One: I like to read. But I'm going to be interrupted. It's a fact. Somebody needs the time, or needs me to move my legs, or my bag, or whatever. I accept that, but if you interrupt me when I'm into a book, I cannot be held responsible for my behavior. A magazine, by comparison, is relatively easy to get in and out of. It's kindness, really, on my part. All wrapped up in my own selfishness.

Two: Magazines often have a hodgepodge of information on a page so if I'm trying to eavesdrop, it doesn't look suspicious if I'm flipping between pages, rather than reading them consecutively.

And Three: It's a barrier. For the most part, people don't strike up a conversation when you appear to be busy. Again, unless you've been blessed with fame and fortune.

On the first leg of my trip home, I was flying from Savannah to Atlanta, where I would catch a connecting flight to St. Louis. I was faking sleep—the most valuable of all crowd coping mechanisms—and the ideal way to listen in on conversations.

I find it cathartic to simply close my eyes, let my other senses take over for a while, and allow my thoughts free rein. I wonder, if we were to find ourselves without a pilot, would I volunteer to land the plane? Am I that heroic? And how would I accomplish that?

Would the control tower be able to guide my frightened passengers and me safely to the ground?

My thoughts skipped to whether or not I would be able to churn butter if I suddenly found myself living on the Frontier, but they were interrupted by … yes, that's what I thought … a slurp, and the sound of a sultry giggle from next door.

That's another reason I shut my eyes on this flight. I felt the need to give the neighboring couple some privacy. Something about them seemed illicit to me and I was mildly repelled. I kept waiting for them to leave—go to the bathroom together, or something. But no, they just stayed seated and kissed each other constantly.

Imagine sitting next to a couple who kiss each other three times. Just three. Imagine it. Three slow, wet, kisses with all the accompanying murmurs and sighs.

By the time I thought to keep count until the plane docked at the gate, I counted thirty-two. My husband didn't kiss me thirty-two times last month.

But worse than their behavior was the sense I kept getting—not from the woman, but from the man—that I was jealous. That if I could have claimed him for my own, I would have. That whole thought was so irritating to me that I shut my eyes and focused on the activity around me.

The group sitting behind me and to the left was discussing a record deal. The woman one row in front of me was mad at her husband—I couldn't hear her perfectly, but I caught her tone, and pieces of sentences. The pilot was trying to be clever through the overhead speakers. The flight attendant was peddling peanuts and coffee on a cart behind me. And the man across the aisle was mumbling to himself.

For me, that much activity is ripe with storytelling potential. Yet I was stuck. Stuck with my eyes shut. Just then, I'd have given everything I owned for a piece of paper, a pen, and the freedom to open my eyes without Rizzo and her boyfriend kicking it up a notch and really trying to impress me.

I think they found it fun to tell themselves I was a teensy bit jealous of their ridiculous behavior, but they were doomed to disappointment. No, what I found fun in the moments I was "awake," was to stare, blank-faced, at their smiles long enough to make them uncomfortable. And after they looked away, I'd cuddle up in my airplane seat, shut my eyes, and smile a little to myself.

PART FOUR:
MARRIAGE

"In passing, also, I would like to say that the first time Adam had a chance, he laid the blame on woman."

~Nancy Astor (1879-1964)
British politician

From: Amy
Sent: Thursday, December 02, 2004 7:18 AM
To: Mona
Subject: Rhythm is my life.

Ringo Rules

Reply
From: Mona

OH – Love Actually. It took me a second to figure out what the hell you were talking about. I like, "I'm Prince William without the weird family." And who else, besides Hugh Grant, could call Margaret Thatcher a "saucy minx"

Reply
From: Amy

Not a soul, I'm afraid. Watched it last night, made Brad watch it with me. Thought he'd pick up on the theme that you need to tell people how you feel now and then. I'm afraid all he walked away with is that goofy British men can get hot chicks in Wisconsin.

CHAPTER FOURTEEN

DAN AND I WERE MARRIED IN the Catholic Church. I don't know if it holds true for other denominations, but before marrying in the Catholic Church couples have to fill out a test—of sorts. The test covers a variety of topics from finance to communication and the man and the woman fill it out separately. The priest collects both sets of answers, they are reviewed by some omnipotent someone, then the couple returns to discuss the findings. Any that you differed from each other, or any answers that were not in line with the Church's expected responses are discussed in this second meeting.

Dan and I were cooking right along until question number one hundred. We answered the same as each other, but our joint answer was in opposition with the Church.

"Number one-hundred," Father Michael began. "You both answered the same, but we need to discuss it."

Dan and I looked at each other, and the priest went on.

"It concerns fidelity, and it reads, 'If my spouse should ever have an extra-marital affair the marriage would be over.' You both answered yes."

He looked at us for confirmation. We both stared at him.

He went on to explain. "The Church would like you to be aware that there are temptations out there, and realize that an affair is oftentimes the result of a deeper issue that has gone unaddressed."

Dan nodded. "Well, sure. That makes sense."

Father looked relieved. "Good. So you recognize that counseling would possibly be in order, and you wouldn't just immediately file for divorce. So I'll ask you again, would the marriage be over if your spouse had an affair?"

We answered in unison. "Yes."

He looked taken aback. "Even if there were children involved?"

"Yes," I answered.

"And if you had found out about the affair ten years after the fact?"

"Yep," said Dan.

"Can I ask your reasoning?"

I answered honestly. "Father, with all due respect to the Church, if Dan had an affair I'd never forget it. I wouldn't even try."

He looked concerned, but said nothing.

"As a matter of fact, I would make snide comments every single chance I got."

I looked to my left, as if speaking to someone: *Do you like this red shirt, Mona?*

Then I turned to the right and answered myself: *I like it better than I liked that affair you had.*

Left: *What do you want for Christmas this year, Mona?*

Right again: *How about a mistress? You know where to get one of those, don't you?*

I turned to the left again and Dan placed a restraining hand on my knee. "That's enough," he said in a low voice.

Father Michael was flipping through his notes, seemingly at a loss for how to respond to such unwavering resolve. Eventually he smiled at us. "Well...don't screw around then! Let's move on..."

So Dan and I had an understanding as we entered into marriage, and I admit, I took it for granted. Until the day I realized that, somewhere between "I do," and "It's a girl," I had lost all the sex appeal I once had.

One day, I went shopping to buy some new clothes, as my entire body had seen fit to reorganize itself since the birth of my daughter, Maggie. My first stop was Victoria's Secret. I had just recently given birth, and I thought I must have been very busty, because everything was falling out every time I leaned over. Very frustrating. Once there, I discovered that my cup had not runneth over, as I had suspected.

"What size are you wearing?" Asked the sales clerk.

"A 34C."

She darted a look from my chest to my face. Then draped the pink tape measure across her shoulders. "Well, that's the problem."

I smiled at her sheepishly. I mean, who would try to stuff these babies into a C-cup?

Then she went on, "You should be wearing a 36B. Everything's falling out because your bra's too big."

Now, all through high school I was a D-cup. After I gave birth to Will, I shrank to a C-cup, which was fine. Now I've pumped my way into a B-cup. Dan and I wanted to have four kids, but the pattern I was seeing was making me rethink that.

After that blow to my ego, I was off to Old Navy to kick my wardrobe up a notch. For some insane reason I decided to try on swimsuits. I guess I thought that since I had suffered through twenty minutes of the exercise bike the day before, I had magically transformed myself into a mean and lean machine. I had not, but I'm sure the guy working the fitting room got a kick out of me laughing uproariously at my reflection behind closed doors.

I looked like the "Before" picture in every bad weight loss ad. Now, don't get me wrong, I don't think I'm fat. I can even stuff and fold myself into a pair of size six pants. I'm just suffering the ill-effects of a recent pregnancy over thirty. There's an injustice to having to gain thirty pounds to spit out a seven pound kid. And anyone who tells you it's balanced out by the beauty of childbirth is lying. So I'm not overweight, I just have a lot of extra skin. People always get mad if I talk about this.

"Oh, Yeah." They'll say, "I feel really bad for you that you're only down to a size six…" Blah, blah, blah.

But I'll tell you like I tell them. Loose skin is unattractive on anybody, whether she's size two or a size twenty-two. And "Dressed Mona" looks a lot better than "Bikini Mona."

While at Old Navy, I picked out some skirts and Capri pants, because I no longer enjoy the sight of myself in shorts. Later, waiting in the checkout line, I was watching people swinging in and out of the front doors. For the most part, it was the young girls who caught my eye. Early out of school for summer break, they were. I couldn't help notice them because of how sharply they contrasted with my own fashionable self.

This morning I managed to get school clothes out of the dryer for Will. I made sure he got in the shower on time and threatened that if he didn't wash his hair well, I would do it for him. I fed Maggie, changed her diaper, and got her dressed. I cooked breakfast, made coffee, and topped it all off with a mad dash out the door to pick up the kids in the carpool and drop them all off at school by half past seven.

My morning routine included all of that, but was suspiciously lacking in the self- grooming department. I did get a brush through my hair, put on deodorant, and brushed my teeth, but I had not a stitch of make-up on. My legs needed to be shaved, so I had to wear jeans on a day when the high temperature reached right around eighty-two degrees.

So I was standing in line, sweating my ass off, and balancing my new clothes on top of the stroller umbrella, seething at these young girls all done up for their big shopping trip. Okay, seething is a strong word. Annoyed is a bit more appropriate.

I was driving home, contemplating which pajama shorts to slide on upon my arrival when I got disgusted.

That's when I started talking to myself. "Do I not care about myself anymore?" I asked aloud. "Would I even be surprised if Dan had an affair?"

It was at my last stop that I realized how far I had fallen.

I went to the gas station to add the first tank of gas to my new car. It was just my luck that the construction crew, building a new church up the road, was hanging around eating lunch. Why they went to the gas station when plenty of fast food restaurants were nearby, I'll never know.

In full view, I pulled up to the pump, parked the car, and went around to fill it up.

Then I realized the gas tank was on the other side. *Damn!*

I got back in the car, and at that point I actually considered leaving. Why? Because I'm so paranoid that I assume people are watching me—even when I have just realized I am no longer watchable. I pulled around to another pump, went back and forth a few times, since I'm not used to lining up the passenger side of the car with the gas pump, then I turned off the engine and got out.

The car looked like a drunken person had parked it, but I was able to pull and swing the gas nozzle over just far enough to precariously balance it in the tank. I had to hold it there, since left to its own devices it would have fallen out, but I refused to move my car a third time.

The hose was stretched to a forty-five degree angle, which I steadfastly ignored in favor of looking very purposeful with my new upper body building regimen.

I was making a scene, and not a particularly welcome one, but all good things—and bad—must come to an end, and this was no exception. I wound up the hose and hung it back up, and as I did so, I dropped my car keys. I bent to pick them up and when I did, I saw it. I was too far away for anyone else to have noticed. But I knew.

I was wearing black socks. With my white tennis shoes.

Black. Socks.

It was then that I decided if Dan had an affair, I would understand completely. I'd never forgive him, and I'd start divorce proceedings faster than he could say "community property." But I'd understand why he did it.

On the flip side, while I expect him to still be charged by me when he gets home in the evening and finds me with dried baby food on my shirt and a headband in my hair, trying desperately to coax some green beans in Maggie's mouth while she's much more interested in blowing it back in my face, I am also supposed to find the energy to get a charge out of him. I don't know. Maybe I should have been turned on when he leaped between me and the TV the night before, wearing only a pair of loose gray boxer shorts he's had since college. Should I have dragged him into the bedroom after that? Was that a mating call, and I didn't answer? Maybe after he eats a quart of ice cream, then pokes his gut, I should be driven wild with anticipation?

It has always bummed me out that falling in love is so easy, and staying in love is so difficult. And sadly, marriage often falls short of the mark. We all get lazy. The initial passion fades. We're not as romantic as we used to be, not as charming, not as irresistible. And let's face it, wanting a man who smiles at you after he burps is not easy. Wanting a woman with stubbly legs and chipped red toe nail polish is no picnic either.

But for all that it falls short from time to time, marriage can also be so much more. Because at the end of the day, it is easy to love a woman who makes you laugh. And it is easy to love a man who, when I complained that by yelling out the window I couldn't get the cricket underneath it to shut up, walks outside and scares it off.

From: Mona
Sent: Wednesday, May 19, 2004 1:17 PM
To: Cathy
Subject:

It's tough to say which part of my life I like best today. Was it the part where Lloyd informed me that if Jessie barked at him one more time he was giving her a—and this is a direct quote—"five finger knuckle sandwich" or was it when he put the door on backwards?

The door, Cath. The one he's been working on for two weeks. You can open it, like, eight inches before it bangs into the heating duct running along the basement ceiling. He came upstairs and said to me, "You got a problem." Then we went downstairs, he showed me the door and I said, "No. You got a problem."

Reply
From: Cathy

Mona! That is so crazy! Why won't Dan just let Jim do it?

Reply
From: Mona

I asked him that. He said, "Lloyd charges twelve bucks an hour! Twelve bucks! I'm not real sure what Jim charges but you can bet for sure it ain't twelve bucks!"

Reply
From: Cathy

When did you marry Archie Bunker?

CHAPTER FIFTEEN

EVERY THURSDAY MORNING DAN GOES TO a business networking meeting. They have some breakfast, talk business, and make speeches about their jobs or the services they provide to the masses. And while public speaking—in front of a group of my peers—is a living nightmare to me, Dan seems to genuinely enjoy it.

The group consists of people from all manner of business: a vitamin salesman, a real estate agent, a masseuse, a florist, Dan's an accountant, and there are many others. At its heart, I tend to think this is a group of salesmen. I think this because ever since he has become a part of it, we've been buying things.

Every month there was something new, something we absolutely had to have. We switched vitamins in March. I was not happy, so that argument raged until late April. By June, we had a new Zoning air conditioner. In the beginning of July, I got new air filters. By August, I had the old ones back. A couple's massage was our gift to each other on our September anniversary. By November, I had received three bouquets from The Mexico Road Florist, and by January we had a top of the line water softener.

Now don't get me wrong, all of these things are wonderful. But we don't need all of them, and we certainly didn't need the highest caliber of them.

If Dan was here, he'd ask me, "Why not? Why not have the best?" And I really don't have an answer to that question. But as soon as Eldon, the water softener guy, tried to sell me soap using the pitch: "You know how soap is really expensive?" Dan knew I had hit my limit. And it stopped for a while—this incessant buying. Then it all came back with the Reverend Lloyd.

We had moved into our new house, and after a brief settling-in period, were ready to make some changes. By the time summer had rolled around, I had already hung wallpaper in the bedroom, installed wainscoting in the bathroom, and painted the kitchen walls. Dan then began more extensive outdoor projects. He ran a waterline out to the shed and replaced the hot water heater. Another project he was contemplating was the removal of a window that was in the basement. He wanted to knock it out and replace it with a door. One night, at dinner, he suggested his idea.

"There's a new guy in our group who's a preacher, but he does handyman work to make extra money and I thought we could hire him for the door downstairs."

I didn't have much to say. "That's fine. You don't think Jim could do it though?" Jim was Dan's friend who owned a construction business. He and his employees were at our house beginning construction on our deck.

"No, I want to get it done before the deck's built," he said.

I shrugged. "Whatever."

"Anyway," he began. "This guy –everything he knows about the handyman business he learned from his dad."

I dipped my knife into the crock of butter. "Wow."

"Yep—" he flipped the cover off the rolls, chose one "—and his dad learned it from his grandpa."

"Hmm. Neat," I murmured distractedly, pushing the butter in his direction.

"I think so," he said.

Dan and I have a lot of similar interests. A good seventy percent of common ground. But the things we each find truly fascinating in life fall into that remaining thirty percent, so we have a lot of conversations that follow that pattern. One person fascinated, the other one bored.

I started to feel bad about my response so I asked, "What's his name?"

"Lloyd."

"Lloyd Dobbler?" I asked.

Dan laughed at my movie reference. "No, I don't know what his last name is."

"Oh," I responded, my attention beginning to wander—

"...but he's black."

Where that jarring segue came from, I'll never know, but nevertheless I looked at Will and yelled, "Hide the silver! There's a black man coming to the house!"

Will looked confused by the outburst, poor kid, and Dan got mad. Partly at me, but mostly at himself. I'm the wrong person to be around when you say the wrong thing, and he knows that.

"Well, I didn't mean it like that…it's just…" He shrugged, at a loss for words. "I don't know…"

"Do we have to pay him?" I prodded.

He looked at me impatiently, "Mona, knock it off. I don't know why I said that. He's a nice guy, okay?"

I held up my hands, "Okay."

"—and I'd just like him put in the door."

"That's fine Dan. I don't care."

The subject was dropped briefly as we made our plates, and Dan asked Will about school. Will fed us only the tiny morsels of information he was willing to part with—but eventually Dan managed to pull out enough information to paint a decent picture of Will's life outside of home. Satisfied, Dan turned the conversation back to where it had been.

"So," Dan interrupted about ten minutes later. "Lloyd's coming over tomorrow to look at it and give us an estimate."

I reached for the spoon and helped myself to the green beans. "I hope he doesn't steal our TV…"

Dan slammed his fork down, and started to leave the table.

I burst out laughing. "Oh, come on!" I coaxed. "I'm kidding… sit back down."

After a tense moment, he did, and I managed to hide my mirth from then on out. Maybe I should have felt bad, but I didn't. It's a flaw of mine, this need to make people realize when they say something uncalled for, or unfair. Lloyd didn't need to be described by his race to me—and certainly not in front of our children—though Heaven knows we, of all races, are guilty of doing it.

Perhaps I was too hard on Dan. After all, and with the exception of my father and step-father, he is the only man I know who does not care about race, creed, sexual orientation, or political affiliation. If he likes someone, he just likes him. To hell with the rest of it.

But don't feel too bad for Dan. This is a man who, when I expressed surprise that the principal of my new school was in a wheelchair, gasped and said, "Do you think he can read?" just to make me feel like a jerk.

I'm an English teacher, so the first thing I noticed about Lloyd the following morning was that that he did—as his driver side door so proudly announced— "Commerical work" as well as Residential. Quickly on the heels of that, I noticed that he talked extremely loud. A booming voice, you might call it. I thought it sounded like the voice of a deaf man.

Lloyd was tall and skinny. As time wore on, I noticed he always wore the same clothes. His work clothes, I imagined. His glasses were too large for his slim face and were always dotted with paint flecks. He smiled a lot, sang a lot, and he loved Lionel Ritchie.

Aside from being one of the friendliest people I have ever had the pleasure of meeting, he had an abrupt manner about him that made him difficult to converse with. He talked *at* me, not *to* me. So, our daily exchanges over the next couple of weeks were more a collection of unrelated sentences rather than complete conversations.

"Hey Lloyd, *The Goonies* is on today." I said one morning.

"Gotta stop at the butcher on my way home." He responded, and sidled closer to the stove. "What're you making?"

I lifted the lid over the pot and he stepped back from the steam.

"Spaghetti sauce…You ever watch *The Goonies*?"

"We're having a potluck this weekend at church." Lloyd was the Reverend down at Christ's Church in the city.

"One-Eyed Willie?" I pressed. "Chester Copperpot? Remember them?"

"The butcher's down on Arsenal."

And I gave up. Uncle. "Whew! That's a drive!"

"You right about that! Yes you are." Then he shook his head and chuckled to himself. Catching sight of Will watching television, he headed next into the family room.

"What're you watching, boy?"

"*The Goonies.*"

He flinched. "Goonie? What's that?"

Will has a poker face like I do, so he looked at Lloyd like he was crazy. "It's a movie."

"What?"

Will spoke louder but his eyes never left the television screen. "Uh…on TV."

"Speak up!"

Even louder, "It's on TV but it's a movie."

"Really?" Lloyd said, full of good will, and genuine interest. Then he'd sit a spell and watch TV with Will. And, standing in the kitchen, I had to wonder:

What exactly did he learn from his dad?

From: Mona
Sent: Wednesday, December 22, 2004 8:49 AM
To: Girls, Matt
Subject: This week in People

....................................My subscription ran out. Crap.

From: Mona
Sent: Wednesday, December 22, 2004 11:35 AM
To: Girls, Matt
Subject: This week in Entertainment

I am utterly bereft without People magazine, but I shall persevere and find my observations elsewhere. Next up: Entertainment Magazine. Three things:
1.Some reporter is trying to analyze why a black man didn't become the next Apprentice. Great. Put another log on that fire.
2.Every time I see a Gap ad I kind of thing Sarah Jessica Parker is in love with herself—and really, why shouldn't she be.
3.And on a sad note...Jessica Shaw reports that my favorite of all tricks, the Silent Treatment is "out." But the good news? Drink Throwing is "in."

Bring on the eggnog!

Merry Christmas,
Mona

CHAPTER SIXTEEN

I'M A CARELESS PERSON. I GUESS that's an accurate assessment. I can afford to be. Not financially, but philosophically. If some catastrophe should ever befall us, I have about three possessions that I truly care about. As long as I have my family, everything else is gravy. Sure, I *want* my things, but I can live without them.

It's easy for me to cut my losses. It's easy for me to leave things behind. Dan doesn't like this about me, steeped as he is in continuity and tradition—holds onto the past, he does, until it fairly strangles him. But, what the hell? Opposites attract, and God knows we're living proof.

Running parallel to this, although it is not the same thing, is my tendency to ruin clothes in the washer. Just because I'm not overly concerned with their demise, does not mean I do it on purpose. Dan tends to overlap the two traits, although they are actually unrelated. Just because I am unmoved by the loss of his green-striped Rugby shirt from 1989, doesn't mean I shrunk it on purpose. I do not set out to leave his clothes in the washer so long that they actually start re-staining each other. And to this day, I'm not sure why I was expected to know that you cannot wash a goose down comforter.

I'm not good at physics, so I can't really explain what happened, physically, to all the feathers inside the comforter. But what we had the night after I washed it, and the three week's worth of nights following, was essentially two sheets, sewn one on top of the other, with a few pockets of shriveled up feathers dotted between.

The duvet cover was buttoned around it. So really, *four* sheets are what separated us from the elements of our room—the "meat locker" as we call it. Seventy-one degrees in our room is not the same seventy-one degrees that hang out in the family room. But none of that is my point.

The point is that, in the end, I had ruined the comforter, and it was up to me to fix it. I tend to take things like that in stride, and I fancy that I take my consequences like a gal should. I saved up Dan's money and I took myself off to the mall for a new one.

If memory serves, it was in January when I went in search of a new comforter, so I was reaping the benefits of the After-Christmas sales. It wasn't long before I found exactly what I was looking for. In one of the department stores I found a King-size Luxury White Goose down comforter for only ninety-nine dollars. About four hundred dollars cheaper than I had ever seen them in the past.

"Look at these deals!" I said to the woman next to me, an action which betrayed my enthusiasm. I am not normally chatty with complete strangers. "Can you believe it?" I shook the package. "A hundred bucks for a comforter!"

She glanced at the sign, and then at me. "Wow," she said without a single drop of excitement. Which is exactly why I don't talk to people I don't know, because they don't want to talk to me either, and it's embarrassing. But that day I didn't care.

"If you're looking for a comforter, you better pick up one of these!" I suggested, but she had already walked away.

There were other items on sale, and I looked around the department for a while, but the comforter was getting progressively heavier, so I headed to the check out counter.

"Can you believe the price of this thing?" I asked the clerk, still awash with excitement. I couldn't wait to tell Lynn. She is a bargain shopper, and is always proud of me when I pick up something for a fraction of its original cost.

The clerk smiled. At least she was friendly. "We've got a pretty good sale going on, don't we?"

"Pretty good?" I chuckled. "This thing is a hundred bucks! I'd say that's pretty good!"

She laughed. I'm good with sales people. I used to be one. I know their job isn't the greatest—especially during the holidays. So I always try to be friendly and light with them, if with no one else.

On my way out the door, I wandered into the shoe department to take off my coat. The strain of carrying a fluffy down comforter—wrapped in yards of plastic—through an overheated shopping mall, while wearing my coat and hat, left me feeling dizzy and slightly nauseated.

While I sat there, I spied a pair of brown leather boots I would have liked to have. I even took the time to try them on, but I had to pass. I just couldn't imagine carrying both packages out to the car, since I had been reduced to carrying the comforter in a bear-hug grip and walking sideways in an effort to see where I was going.

Shopping in the middle of a Missouri winter is always an uncomfortable chore. The temperature on the inside of the mall is as stifling as the outside temperature is bitter. But, no matter how close you park to the mall entrance, you cannot leave your coat in the car. The temperatures hover just below freezing, and the wind is piercing and damp coming off the Missouri River.

When I made it home, I went straight to work. I stripped the bed, put on fresh sheets, and slid the duvet cover over the new comforter. The duvet was a bit longer than the comforter, but it didn't matter to me. What mattered was that my new cover was thick. So thick, that it seemed to add a good three inches of height to the mattress, and so lush and cozy that I couldn't resist the opportunity to lay back and rest my weary arms.

When Dan got home that night, I couldn't wait to show him. I rushed him back to the bedroom and he studied it. He has to study everything meticulously before offering an opinion, which always ruins my excitement a little. Just once I would like an instant reaction from him. Instant excitement. Instant delight.

Dan also has a knack for noticing the *one* thing that's wrong. I could paint an entire room beautifully, and he will look at it and see the spot of paint I got on the ceiling. Will could clean his entire room, and Dan would look at it and see the sock left under the dresser. If there was one thing I could change about Dan, it would be that aspect of his personality. He has a way of making people feel like they've never done a job that's quite good enough.

As the years go by, I see him trying to correct this quality, or at least soften it. But excellence—the first time around—has been so ingrained in him since childhood, that I don't think he would know how to completely change it, even if he wanted to. I watched him walk to the bed and pinch the extra fabric surrounding the comforter. Finally, he spoke. "Is this outside cover too big?"

"It is a little," I admitted, "but it'll shrink." Especially if I wash it.

He looked like he didn't believe me. "What size is it?"

"It's a King, Dan!" I spat out. "Just like the duvet cover is."

God, I hated him sometimes. Just because I understood the roots of his personality didn't mean he couldn't make me spit fire. While I leaned on the door jam and watched him through narrowed eyes, he continued to marvel at the difference in sizes. He picked up the edge of the comforter and looked underneath it. Then he stood, went over to the other side and did it again. Finally, he stood upright and shook his head.

"It's weird, though…"

"It's fine!" I said. "This is how some things are..." Which made no sense at all, but that's a little idiosyncrasy of mine. When I'm embarrassed or unsure about something, I overcompensate by acting like a know-it-all.

He smiled up at me, completely oblivious to the emotion churning in the room. "Oh, I know...it's just..." he shrugged, "I don't know, it just looks wrong."

"Well, not everything is perfect all the time, Dan!" I snapped. "I know that's hard for you to understand—"

"But...it's, like, seven inches longer than the comforter..."

"Then take it back!" I shouted over my shoulder and walked away. "Take it back if it's not good enough!"

Moments later, as I stood in the kitchen, stewing, I couldn't help but sympathize with the woman who used to watch Will after school for a couple of hours each day. She would often answer the door with a harried expression on her face and announce—without preamble—"If I look like I'm pissed off, it's because I'm married to a horse's ass!"

That night, in bed, Dan snuggled next to me under the covers. "Ooh, it's warm."

I smiled at him through the darkness. This is what he does. If he doesn't ever say the word "sorry," well at least he finds something to say to make me feel better. He leaned over and kissed me. "Thanks for getting it. I know you went out of your way."

I huddled under more, letting the warmth seep into my body. "It's so nice to be warm in here again, and not have all those other little blankets all spread out."

"I know!" He agreed. "That drove me crazy!"

We had taken to adding other blankets and throws on the bed to stave off hypothermia, but it only provided a source of unending exasperation. Nothing fit right. They overlapped, bunched up, and you had to choose which body parts to cover.

When I was almost asleep, he spoke again. "Boy, this is a heavy blanket."

"It is, but it's nice."

"Yeah. It is."

The next night Dan and I were still puzzled by the weight of our new blanket. Dan flipped to the side, and exhaled loudly. "What is it about this blanket? Why is it so heavy?"

"I don't know. Last night I tried to go to the bathroom and I could hardly get out of bed..." I could feel Dan turn to face me in the dark and I needed no further encouragement. "I swear, I pushed it twice and it kept flipping back on me...like it was attacking me or something..."

Dan hid his face in the pillow as soon as he started laughing. He always does—as if he doesn't want to laugh, but can't help himself.

"...finally, the third time, I threw it back and made a run for it."

I lifted my head off of the pillow, and shoved his shaking form. "You laugh…but it was frightening…"

That only served to set off another round of helpless amusement from his side of the bed.

The next morning, Dan announced that he had hardly slept at all—claimed he felt pinned to the mattress. I didn't disagree. I couldn't breathe under it. Unfortunately, the strain of getting it back into the plastic bag required more strength than I knew I had, and a capacity for profanity that had gone previously untapped. But, soon I was on my way back to the mall. Back to return my fabulous bargain before it killed us.

"Hi." I expelled on a heavy breath once I made it to the checkout counter at the mall. I dropped my return to the floor with a thud, and reached in the back pocket of my jeans for the receipt. I smiled at the cashier and placed it on the counter. "How are you today?"

She glanced up. "I'm good." Then over the counter and down at my feet. "What'cha got down there? A return?" She motioned for me to bring it to the side of the counter.

I lifted it in front of me with two hands and duck-walked over to her.

"Man," I said as I paddled over. "This thing is so heavy! There's nothing wrong with it, it's just too heavy."

She turned it from side to side. Some sort of inspection process. I assumed that I—or it—passed, because she turned back and grabbed my receipt.

"I mean, it must be really high quality, because my husband and I could hardly breathe under it. I guess we're just not high quality people." I gave a short laugh.

Sure, not my best joke—a fact which she made readily apparent—but it didn't deserve the look I got, either. Nevertheless, I pressed on. "It also was a lot shorter than the duvet cover. Are they sized differently at different places, do you know?"

She threw me a fleeting look. "No. Mattress sizes are pretty universal. Can I see the card you used to purchase this?"

"Oh! Sure..." I dug in my purse. "Man, that's weird though. Is it possibly marked wrong?"

"No, it's a King." Another look. I was trying to be friendly, but this woman was not making it easy.

"Gosh, that's weird." I wasn't saying she was wrong, and I kept my smile in place, but the whole thing was strange. I tried to remember where I had bought the duvet cover. Maybe *that* was sized wrong. But it had fit perfectly over our last comforter.

I tried to explain it more clearly. "It was just...I mean, this comforter was a good—" I held my hands out at a distance from each other. "A good seven, eight inches smaller than the duvet...maybe the duvet was sized wrong—"

"Ma'am?" she interrupted me.

I stopped with my hands hanging in mid air.

"That's not a comforter, it's a mattress pad."

I dropped my hands onto the counter. "Oh..." was all I could think to say.

It took me a second to assimilate that new information...but when it finally clicked, I let out a peal of laughter that I'm sure they could hear clear over in Outdoor Apparel.

I stood at the counter and laughed until I thought my ribs would crack. I laughed as I signed the return receipt. I laughed all the way to the car. I laughed so hard that I could barely tell Dan the story when I called him at work. And to this day, when he tells the "mattress pad" story—always a party favorite—I laugh so hard that I cannot even catch my breath.

From: Dan
Sent: Thursday, August 11, 2005 11:32AM
To: Mona
Subject: Jury Duty

When that jury duty letter comes in, let me know ASAP.

Thanks. Dan

Reply
From: Mona

Okay, I tried to call you but you couldn't get to the phone. I got your jury duty thing in the mail and here's what it says:

Dear Mr. I-Think-I'm-Better-Than-The-Judicial-System,

We have received your notice and, no, you cannot weasel out of jury duty for the second time this year. You think you've got deadlines? So do we. We need to get these rapists and murderers off the streets. Have you ever taken a civics course, sir? Jury duty is not some crazy punishment we've designed to inconvenience you. No, it's something we employ to allow you to perpetuate this little thing we call Democracy..."

Just kidding. They're moving it to sometime in the next 6 months.

You're welcome. Mona

CHAPTER SEVENTEEN

I THINK IT WILL COME AS no surprise to anybody when I announce that men and women cannot ever get along for any length of time. Well, any two people, really. So long as you're talking, you're bound to disagree.

The most enjoyable thing about marriage is that you get to practice arguments. As if it's one big movie and it requires fifteen takes to really nail a scene. You fight about the same thing over and over and over...until eventually, you no longer need the script. You both know your lines by heart. And if either party has brought children into the union—then the gloves are off. Go to your separate corners, wait for the bell, and come out swinging.

But Dan and I have been married almost four years. The turf war that was our first two years of marriage has passed. We have hammered out how to raise, treat, and look at the children. I do miss the Honeymoon feeling a bit sometimes, but I wouldn't go back and relive those two years if somebody paid me a gazillion dollars.

So now that Dan and I are past the huge blow-ups and all the fights that neither of us won, we're down to the nitty-gritty. The picky stuff. The boring stuff.

No one fights about the garage door when they're dating, but just recently Dan and I had an argument about that very thing. He swears that raising and lowering the garage door uses more electricity than leaving a light on for two days "or something"—he's not real into specifics.

Dan has this weird thing about electricity, and it's an odd thing for me not to share since I'm so concerned about recycling and the environment and such. But while I could care less about that damn garage door, that's the proverbial hill Dan's willing to die on.

This is what our life has boiled down to. Electricity.

I feel like I'm married to my grandpa. What I wouldn't give to go back in time armed with the information that it does *not* actually cost money to make a local call! Rats!

One night I was making chocolate chip cookies and listening to *Country Music Television*. I often have *CMT* on, just as background noise. It annoys Dan, but I think it's nice. For me it's a throwback to childhood. We always had a television on somewhere. As throwbacks go, it's not bad. He ought to be thankful I'm not knocking back a bottle of Gin and running around the block in clogs. That's a little nugget I could have picked up from certain family members—who shall remain nameless—but I didn't.

At any rate, in the absence of anything else, I always have *CMT* on. I like to sing along. I don't need to see it to enjoy it. It's the same with the news. I listen to it—I don't necessarily sit there and stare at the screen.

But Dan must not have understood that, because he walked in the family room that evening, picked up the remote, and turned the channel. Bam. Just like that.

I protested. "Hey! I was listening to that."

"To what?"

"The TV. I like to listen to the TV when I'm cooking."

He looked disbelieving. "In the kitchen?"

"Yes. In the kitchen. Turn it back."

"You're not even watching it." He infuriated me more by searching through the Guide at the bottom of the screen.

"Well, I'm not a Neanderthal. I don't need to see the TV to enjoy what's on it." I threw my arms out in a wide expansive gesture. "Look at me! I can bake cookies and listen to the TV at the same time!" I wished I knew any circus tricks. Because, I tell you what, I would have juggled that cookie dough if I could have. Instead I just said, in my best ring-leader voice, "Yes folks, step right up and watch Multi-Tasking at its finest!"

Dan was staring at me, not at all impressed. "It was *CMT* right?"

"Yes."

He motioned with the remote toward the radio in the kitchen. "You want to listen to country music, turn the radio on."

I shot back. "Or you could just turn it back to the show I was watching!"

"No you weren't! There were no videos on!"

"I know, but I was listening to it." I scooped up a ball of dough and slammed it on the cookie sheet. "It's the Warren Brothers. One of their wives is pregnant." Ha.

"Jesus." He mumbled and I got mad. I stalked over to him and grabbed the remote. "So you just walk into a room where there's a TV on—"

He grabbed it back. "That nobody was watching."

"—and change the channel? You don't think it's rude of you not to ask?"

"Not if nobody's in the room. And why are you watching it, when you could just turn on the radio. You know you're wasting electricity."

This was crazy. "Oh we're worried about electricity, are we?" I gestured down the hallway. "Why don't you go turn out your office light, then, if you're so damn concerned about the environment?"

He turned his back on me, walked to his chair and reclined to watch "Band of Brothers."

I walked over and stood next to him.

He focused hard on the TV screen.

I waved my hand in front of his face. "Hello?"

That didn't faze him so I went on. "So you don't think you're just being totally rude right now?"

"No. But I think you are."

"I think you know you're wrong and that's why you're trying to change the subject."

That may have been stretching it. Changing the subject implied he was still speaking to me, and he wasn't. But I went on like the little trooper I am. "Maybe you should just say you're sorry."

He slammed his chair back upright and said, "Fine." He put down the remote. "Here. I'll go watch TV in the other room."

I accepted his apology, such as it was, then I picked up the remote and changed the channel.

"Thank you." I said. I was talking to myself though, because he had already walked into the bedroom and slammed the door—which put me in quite a quandary. Earlier in the week Will had done the same thing. That brought me, briefly, to another thought. *Why were people always slamming doors in my face?*

After Will's feudal display of power, I had said nothing. But when Dan came home that evening, I greeted him with, "I need you to take Will's door off the hinges."

"Okay." My announcement didn't even break his stride. Nothing I say surprises him anymore.

"Where do you want me to put this door?" Dan asked after he had completed my request. I was standing at the bottom of the stairwell being as helpful as you can imagine I ever am. I yelled up my answer.

"Leave it right there. Right next to the hinges, so he sees it every day and remembers that he can't shut it."

Unfortunately, when Dan slammed the door behind him after our little argument, Will had just come down the steps. He stood there, frozen, with his box of LEGOs. Then he looked at me and said, "He just slammed the door."

I swung my gaze from the bedroom door to him and confirmed. "Yes I see that."

I was momentarily tempted to take our door off its hinges just for the comic value, but I needed Dan's help with that, and he didn't seem to be in the mood for comedy.

I envisioned the battle for the door if I attempted the undertaking myself, but no matter which way I sliced it, the struggle always ended with one of us getting smacked in the forehead with the door. And while there's no doubt I wanted to hit him with something, it wasn't a door.

The following day was Saturday and I was watching *The Karate Kid* with Will in the family room as I fed Maggie in her bouncer seat. I was watching the movie off and on, wishing fervently that Ralph Macchio would have married me like I wanted him to in the seventh grade. Instead I was married to the Door Slammer who still hadn't said a word to me since he left to cut the grass that morning, or I to him.

I sighed and confessed my secret to Will. "I loved him when I was in grade school."

"Who?"

"Ralph Macchio." I motioned toward the television. "That guy. The karate guy in the movie."

Will was horrified. "That guy?"

"No, not him. The young guy. I had pictures of him all over my wall…well the wall Grandma let me put pictures on…"

"Do you still love him?"

"No, I love Dan." But I must have sounded less than pleased with my life's choices.

"Dan knows karate." Will offered.

I shook my head. "But he's no karate kid." I picked up Maggie and carried her into the den to change her diaper and put her down for nap. I came back into the family room to find Dan changing the channel. Again. I must have made some kind of noise because he glanced up from the TV and looked at me.

"You're doing it again." I breathed.

Will glanced up at Dan. "Told ya…"

This time Dan did look sorry. Sorry I busted his ass. "Oh!" He said all wide-eyed innocence. "I thought you were in the other room."

My voice was on the rise. "I went in there to change Maggie's diaper."

Suddenly in an awful hurry, he said, "Sorry!" and changed the channel back. He set the remote down and, patted it— tap, tap, tap— like a peace offering. Then he headed for the door. I shouted after him, "I walked out of the room for five freaking seconds!" He never answered. The next thing I heard out of him was the weed whacker.

Smart man.

An hour passed, and found us in much the same positions as the previous evening. I was in the kitchen, but reading, not cooking. Dan had just kicked back in the chair and clicked on the television. Just in time to catch the tail end of *The Karate Kid*.

He must have learned his lesson because he hollered into the kitchen, "You watching this?"

I looked up from my book, confused. "Watching what?"

"*The Karate Kid.*"

"Was the TV on?"

"Mona," he said in a tone that may have sounded patient to the untrained ear, but I could tell he was getting irritated. "You were watching the Karate Kid earlier. Are you still watching it?"

"Was the TV on?" I asked again.

Dan gets real bent out of shape if you don't understand him the first time he says something—even if he's standing sixteen yards away and yelling into the wind, so I imagine the fact that I couldn't definitively answer a question he posed across the length of the family room was grating to his nerves. And I imagine this because here's how he asked his question for the third time:

"Are. You. Still. Watching. The. Karate. Kid?"

But I had a point to prove. "Was. The. T. V. On?"

For a moment he was silent. "Well, now I don't remember," he admitted.

I smiled to myself, but I didn't respond. I'm a smart girl too.

PART FIVE: RAISING CHILDREN

"There's a time when you have to explain to your children why they're born, and it's a marvelous thing if you know the reason by then."

~Hazel Scott (1920-1981)
Trinidad-born American musician

From: Mona
Sent: Wednesday, January 5, 2004 1:35 PM
To: Girls, Matt
Subject: Wheeling and Dealing

*I got a call from Mrs. Kowalczak (the school principal)
today that Will and Nathan were "wheeling and dealing"
in the bathroom. Apparently Nathan was selling Will a
Revolutionary war coin for ten dollars. The coin, of course,
has no monetary value. I can't wait for the big spender to
get home so I can sell him a penny for five bucks. Both boys
are in the office. The coin and the ten dollar bill have been
confiscated and will be returned at the end of the day.*

Reply All
From: Cathy

*Will does no wrong! That Nathan kid must be bad news.
Maybe the coin is actually from the Russian Revolution, not
the American, as Will originally suspected. Well, I'm sure
it's well worth the ten dollars, or rubles, whatever currency
they're comfortable using on the black market.*

Reply All
From: Amy

*So the Revolutionary War coin is going that high on the
Bathroom Market. I'll go dig up my Confederate War Bonds
and see what I can get for them.*

Reply All
From: Matt

*Someone should tell Mrs. Kowalwolzokjafdosial that
"wheeling and dealing" is what makes the world go round.*

Reply All
From: Lynn

*They called to tell you this?…and who actually witnessed the
wheeling and dealing anyway? What a snitch.*

Reply All
From: Mona

*I sat down with Will and gave him these great words of
wisdom:*
"Nothing good was ever bought in a bathroom."

CHAPTER EIGHTEEN

MOST OF THE TIME, I'M NOT sure if my son is a head case or a bona fide genius.

He is a fabulous artist, and while that is wonderful, I find that it puts his head up in the clouds more times than I care to count. He will often be asked to do a certain chore, and I'll find him ten minutes later doing something completely different.

"Oh. I forgot." He'll say. He'll always say.

It took me three days of campaigning to convince him that, no, he could not make a set of "Doc Ock" arms for the Science Fair. When he finally conceded he said, "That's okay. I was a little nervous anyway about hooking it up to my spine."

Here of late, he wants to create a robot that will do his chores for him. I made him pinky swear that he wouldn't try to "invent" electricity. So when he told me he had auditioned for a part in the school Christmas play, I was understandably nervous. I know him. I worried he would be picturing the robot, imagining his blissfully idle new life, and miss his cue on stage.

On our way out the door the night of the play, Will couldn't find his gloves. In a rush, I yelled for him to "Just find something and get in the car." He grabbed a pair of mittens and rushed outside.

When the third grade class at St. Thomas School filed onto the stage, they wore gloves and hats in order to look like Christmas Carolers. When it came time for Will's line, he did beautifully. He knew just when to speak. He spoke loudly and clearly and with just the right amount of emotion. I should have saved my concern for the moments after his line.

Will went back to his place, and he and his classmates began a new song. It had hand movements that went along with it. Not that he could tell what they were. He was about a half motion behind everyone else, which isn't all that unusual. Add in the fact that he was preoccupied by his neighbors and it's going to be a problem.

He was annoyed that he had to stand next to Cameron, a boy who, in Will's words, "Has a voice that makes the whole song sound wrong." On his other side was a girl named Lisa who was born for the spotlight. Lisa takes dance lessons, so she had every word and every single hand motion down pat. Unfortunately for Will, the hand motions were such that Lisa's hand came in regular contact with his chin and upper torso.

I looked over at Dan, who was laughing quietly.

"Look at him." He said. "You know he paid just enough attention in practice to know when his cue was and then just turned it off. That cracks me up."

At the end of the song, when the students had to put their hands out in a "ta-da!" motion, Will became fascinated with how his hand looked in a mitten. While his hands were in front of him he started bending and flexing his right hand. When all of the students lowered their hands, he stayed as he was.

He studied his hand.

He pumped his arms up and down.

He wiggled his fingers. Then his wrist.

In the silence before the next number his friend Daniel finally leaned over and smacked his hand. And that brought Will back to reality, back to the gymnasium on that cold night a week before Christmas, where we were all anxiously awaiting the next act.

From: Mona
Sent: Monday, September 08, 2003 3:20 PM
To: Girls
Subject: Last Night in the Emergency Room

Hey girls. Just had to tell you that Will had to get six stitches on his chin last night. He hit a parked car when he was riding his bike, and his chin broke his fall when he flew onto the hood.

I'm sure we were quite a sight in the hospital. Will had one doctor, two nurses and Dan at the head of the bed with him. I had one nurse at the foot of the bed with me the whole time going, "Its okay, Mom..."

I suppose this is my penance for laughing at Bridget (for hitting a parked car) and Amy (for using her face to break her fall) too much.

He's fine. I'm not.
Mona

Reply
From: Amy

Let Will know that Chris O'Donnell—a.k.a. Batman's sidekick Robin—also has a chin scar. So he's in good company. (I don't know the details of how Chris got his scar; just noticed it when drooling over him in The Bachelor. I think it makes him even MORE dreamy.)

Hang in there, Mom. Only 60 more years or so of this worrying-about-your-kid stuff.

Reply
From: Mona

Just what a 7 year old boy wants... to be dreamy.

CHAPTER NINETEEN

"FINE!" THAT'S WILL'S NEW FAVORITE WORD. And my new least favorite.

I once read somewhere: "A parent's only job during any of the phases of adolescence is to get their children through it alive." When I read that, I thought the author was referring to drinking and driving and drugs—all the usual suspects. Now I think he was referring to my daily urge to commit murder.

However, I do realize that one of the most important jobs of a parent is to be able to exercise restraint when your child needs it. Compassion. Understanding. So when Will busted out his new favorite word for the second time in the same morning, I let it go. But I sent him a look, warning him that he was standing on a patch of very thin ice.

Dan looked at me for direction. He always does with the kids. Dan, who can juggle clients at work, deal expertly with the IRS, run two farms, and knows how to fix an antique tractor, is mildly frightened by the many moods of our own two children.

Dan raised an eyebrow when Will slammed the cereal box on the table, but waited silently for my lead. I shook my head. *Don't engage.* Then I poured my first cup of coffee.

I knew Will was just really depressed. Goldie had died the night before. Goldie the fish. Will has, or rather, *had* two fish, Goldie and Mr. Doodles. For his tenth birthday I had bought him a fish tank with all the trappings. Will picked out two fish a couple of days later to complete the gift, and all of this was above the objections of Dan who said fish are a pain in the ass. He's right. They are. And it's the only time Dan has it on record that I was wrong and he was right.

I remember that Goldie died on a Thursday. I would never say it to Will, but I think it's all his friend Alex's fault. We took Alex with us to the Lincoln County Fair—an experience I could have done without—but country singer Trace Adkins was there, and if you knew my husband at all, you'd know we had to be there too.

When it was finally time to round up the boys, we found them over by the roller coasters.

"Hold on!" Alex yelled over the roar. Then he and Will disappeared briefly into a crowd that had been drinking for the better part of seven hours. They came back in a timely manner. Alex was carrying a plastic bag, and in it, a fish. A mean beady-eyed little bastard, but I didn't comment.

It came to pass, by the end of the night, that Will and I were the proud fish-sitters of a baby fish, as Alex and his family were going on vacation the following morning. Fabulous!

On the day before Alex was due to pick up the fish (who I had named Bastard), he was found floating in the aquarium filter. We flushed him down the toilet, Will saluted him as he made his final lap, and our only concern was for Alex's feelings at that point. But really, how attached could he have been? He knew Bastard for about forty-five minutes before he surrendered him to our expert care.

Bastard's death was followed by Goldie a short forty-eight hours later. I knew Goldie was dead the second Will came downstairs and called my name.

A person's voice takes on a certain tone when they're trying to sound reasonable yet have alarming news to impart. And sometimes I think mothers are the only ones who can hear it. Dan's voice contained this quality when Will fell off his bike a few years back and needed stitches. The two of them came in the front door, and Dan called up the stairs.

"Mona?"

Hearing his tone, my heart stopped. I ran downstairs to find them. Dan with a steadying hand on Will's shoulder. Will with his hand on his chin, blood mixing with tears, and dripping through the cracks of his fingers.

"Goldie's dead," Will choked, his eyes dry and huge. Then he ran back upstairs to keep watch. Dan thinks Bastard had a disease. I think Bastard's dead body let off some sort of toxic something-or-other and killed Goldie. Goldie's death was a bit more tragic to Will. He picked out Goldie. To him, Goldie was part of the family.

After spending a brief time entertaining Dan by playing Taps on my pretend bugle, I headed upstairs to find Will sitting, cross-legged, in front of his tank. He was staring at Goldie, willing him back to life. I walked quietly to his side.

"He's just floating." He said and impatiently dashed a tear. Three words, and my heart broke for him. Because who am I to judge how he felt about those disgusting fish?

I suggested that maybe it was something in the water. We took Mr. Doodles out, as a precautionary measure, and put him in the fish bowl we reserve for the days we clean the tank. Then we fished out Dead Goldie and set him in an empty Batman box.

We set off for the pond in our backyard. Dan, appropriately melancholy, handed me a flashlight for our trip down the hill, and I dutifully took it.

The procession began. Down the deck steps. Down the hill. Over the bridge, down to the bank of the pond. Me with the flashlight, Will with the Batman box, Goldie with his earthly remains.

Skip and Jessie, our Labs, eventually filled in behind us and rounded out our procession. Dan stayed back with the baby and watched from the deck.

It occurs to me, now, that Heads of State don't have funerals that meaningful.

Upon reaching the pond, Will found it important to find just the right spot to fling our dead friend and I resisted the urge to rush him. People tend to focus on different details when faced with death. When Dan's dad died, his sister refused to get rid of his lawnmower, even though she lived in Connecticut, and we had no use for it here. My mom wanted a certain plant from my grandfather's funeral, and she would not rest until she got it.

And just because Dan focused his energy on different aspects of their father's death, and I honed in on a different plant from Grandpa's wake, doesn't make any person's need any greater or any weaker at a time like that.

So even though this was only a fish to me—and a disgusting one at that—his death broke a part of Will's heart.

"Should we say a few words?" Will asked quietly after he disposed of Goldie, and I thank God the laugh that bubbled in my throat never materialized.

"Uhh…sure," I said and bowed my head.

He glanced up at me. "You go first."

"Oh!" I was surprised. "Okay. Well, he…" I cleared my throat, "…he was a good fish. A good swimmer…"

Will closed his eyes and pinched the bridge of his nose.

Concerned, I kept an eye on him as I went on. "Uhhh...He always—"

But my words were cut off by Will's low sound of distress. "This is going to make me cry," he said and stepped away to compose himself. I used the time to compose myself as well, although not from crying. It was terribly difficult. I'm a nervous laugher. I laugh when I'm supposed to be silent. I laugh when I'm supposed to be serious. But I was all too aware of the importance of not laughing at this. Not laughing at him. And I would have bitten my tongue in half rather than let that happen.

Soon he came back. "Okay. Go on." I reached out and hugged him to me. He started to push away, the boy in him wrestling with the man, but for tonight at least, the boy won. He stopped pushing and leaned in to my side.

I looked down at him. "Do you want to say something?"

"He was a good friend to Mr. Doodles," was his muffled comment.

I patted his shoulder. "Yes, he certainly was."

"And he seemed to like Alex's fish."

Right up until he killed him, was my immediate thought, but what I said was, "Yes, he was very friendly." Thank God.

We stood there in silence for a moment. Every now and then, he lowered his head, and tugged on the edge of my sweatshirt. I didn't comment. There are no words for the moments you watch your child struggle between who he used to be and who he has to become. When I watch him hold back tears, or covertly wipe his eyes, I am grateful he is taking those steps. For his sake. The world is not kind to boys who won't become men. But there's a part of me that wants to cry right along with him. I know the pain in your throat when you're trying to be strong. I know the frustration at tears that won't stop falling. So I stood there, silent in the darkness, and let him pretend he wasn't crying.

And while I hated those fish, and have wished them dead in a hundred different ways on past nights, that night I knew I'd find myself praying. Praying that Will doesn't cry himself to sleep. Praying that Mr. Doodles is alive come morning. Praying that, next time, Will wants a hamster.

From: Mona
Sent: Friday, January 27, 2006, 8:37 AM
To: Dan
Subject: upcoming dates

Mike and Jane's wedding is the 4th of November. Did you know that? Well, write it on your calendar. Also, I will be in Cape Cod with the girls from Sept. 21-24, so any dove hunting plans will have to be put on hold, mister. And remember Amy and Brad's wedding is October 7th. Love you. Mona.

Reply
From: Dan

Let me check my schedule: Nov 4-bowhunting, Sept 21-24, bowhunting/dove hunting, Oct 7th - bowhunting, Dec 1st - sign divorce papers, Dec 2nd - More hunting. But I am totally impressed you know that dove season starts in Sept.

Reply
From: Mona

Are you kidding? I worked in Silex. I didn't have half of my students until nine o'clock during dove season...or turkey season...then there was bow season...rifle season...deer season...God forbid there was an extended doe hunt somewhere...
But hunting season is SO SHORT ...or so you would have me believe.

Oh, I just noticed the "sign divorce papers" part. You're pretty funny for a dead man.

CHAPTER TWENTY

ANY TEACHER WILL TELL YOU THE weeks, and then days, leading up to Christmas vacation are a curious combination of wonderful and horrible. Some tend to think Mondays are the worst. I say Fridays are— the weekend is so close you can almost touch it, one more week down. Yet still, you have to struggle through the next eight hours with all of your students, who are almost as excited about vacation as you are.

For two years I worked at a school called St. Andrew's in a small town in Missouri. It was a funny little place; steeped in small town politics and run by the most honest, hard-working people I have ever had the pleasure of knowing.

One particular Friday morning I entered the school office to find Mrs. Mueller seated behind the typewriter.

I stopped in the doorway. "What are you doing here?"

"Can't come in on Monday, so I wanted to help out today."

Ann Mueller helped in the school office every single Monday, but only if she was asked. She had done this every Monday for the past eight years, and only because every single Friday somebody called and requested her services.

"Well that was nice of you. Have you been having a nice week?"

"Well, I guess. I got so much to do. You know my granddaughter's having a baby, feels like every time I turn around I'm buying another gift and going to another party."

"Oh, if that isn't the truth," I laughed. "When my girlfriend Lynn had her baby, it was like that too. Party, after party, after party." We fell into a brief silence while I read through the Church bulletin and she tapped the keys of the ancient typewriter. Then I asked, "How's your husband doing?"

Ann sat with her back to the computer screen. "Oh, fine, I suppose. He doesn't like this damp though, you know..."

I knew no such thing but said, "No, I don't imagine he does."

"And how was your concert?" She asked me. "I imagine that's what's wrong with your voice."

After I pushed all the necessary keys for a morning math assignment, the copier roared to life. I stepped into the employee bathroom to search through the medicine cabinet.

"Oh Ann, it was awesome," I said in a voice loud enough to carry. "I about had a heart attack I was so excited..."

After washing the aspirin down with a handful of water, I wiped my mouth and returned to stand by the copier. I watched Ann as she blew on a dab of correction fluid and then concentrated on rolling the typewriter spool perfectly back into place.

"Good thing you didn't go with me." I said.

She stopped long enough to shoot me a quick look of disbelief. "Why?"

"Are you kidding? Because he'd have taken you home with him, that's why, and I'd have to be jealous."

She laughed out loud at that—which of course was my goal—since she never laughed out loud at anything, "Girl, I can't hardly keep up with you," she said and shook her head.

When the copier completed its job, I grabbed my copies and the contents of my "mailbox," which was really just a stack tray with my name taped to it, and tucked it all into the crook of my arm.

"Well, I'm off to earn a living!"

Ann's only response was a distracted wave of her hand.

I am a creature of habit, and as such, I had a specific routine at work from which I rarely strayed. Stop Two in my routine was the kitchen and, more specifically, the coffee machine. On the way, I passed a few students and received a few mumbled greetings.

Once in the kitchen, I turned on the lights with a snap and began making coffee. This was my favorite time of the morning. I enjoyed the feeling that the school wasn't really awake yet either. The morning sun was only just beginning to warm the front windows, and the ceiling fans were gearing up for their lazy job of circulating the stale air.

Soon enough, the hall lights would be flipped on by an innovative someone and a flood of students would come pouring in the front door. But for the moment, the hall was silent. Waiting. And the few early students were sleepy and still.

The squeak of the back door interrupted my search for the coffee cups.

"Morning Mona-girl. Cups are in the cabinet on the left. How are you?"

In walked Rosemary Mudd. Mrs. Mudd the Greater I called her. She called me Mrs. Mudd the Lesser. We were not actually related in any way, although we shared a name. Ours was a common last name in the small farming community where I worked. My husband's family hailed from this particular town which made me luckier than most, since I had an "in" to a community that still thought you were new in town ten years after you started calling it home.

Something about Rosemary always made me smile. She was at her make-upped and perfumed best this morning. Her white hair perched like a hard little cloud around her head.

"Well, I am just fine, ma'am. How are you?"

It took a truly courageous person to lay that question on her since Rosemary loved to talk more than anything. In the absence of any new stories, she would just tell the old ones over and over. To say that I loved her stories would be a stretch; she had a way of making a short story long. Rather, I loved to watch her tell a story. She was always so busy. Flitting around. Straightening forks, emptying bags, filling pots with water, and the whole time she'd prattle on, without breaking her stride. And it was a good thing I liked to listen to her as well, because Rosemary wasn't about to give a person a "Fine, thanks" and go on with her day. No. You learned fast not to ask the woman how she was unless you had the time to hear it.

"Well, I'm hot."

This she announced by flapping the front of her shirt and exhaling loudly a few times. Rosemary did double duty as the cook and the bus driver. The poor woman was either in a stifling bus or working hard in front of a hot stove. She ran a tight ship in both places, but still always managed to be mad at somebody, and God love her for it.

I poured my coffee, contemplated mainlining it, but settled for leaning on the counter and drinking it. Fast. While I did this, I watched Rosemary dart around the kitchen in preparation for her day.

"… So then I said, 'Well Bob, if your hand is bothering you, you better let me get that.' So he did. You know he hurt it the last time we were over there. Remember? When Steve and his wife moved into that place off Highway BB? I remember it because we was getting out of the car…"

I interrupted, "I remember." Sometimes it helped to move the conversation along. "How do they like their new house?"

"Oh they love it. I hate to have them so far away though." Then she caught sight of someone in the doorway. "Oh! Good Morning, Mrs. Lenk."

"Good Morning Rosemary. Got any plans this evening?"

"Well, I was just telling Mona-girl, here. We're going to the new house this weekend…"

With that, I snuck out to gather my students. I'd have to get the rest of that story later.

As I walked out of the kitchen I noticed the lights on in the hall. Down the way a locker slammed. Further down, a toilet flushed.

And while the cafeteria had been only occupied by a few bleary-eyed students when I had passed it last, it was now abuzz with a hundred little conversations.

I stood at the door and hollered over the din. "Seventh and Eighth grade!" And the students in my small class stood, slung their bags over their shoulders and formed a line in front of me. I said nothing to any of them until they formed the kind of line I like to see. Then I smiled. "Go on down." I motioned for them to walk down the hall. All ten of them. That was seventh and eighth grade combined.

St. Andrew's was a rural school with an entire student body of fifty-nine, from Kindergarten through Eighth grade. But don't go thinking the small size diminishes the teacher's job, because it doesn't. It only scales it back a bit.

The fact remains, there are only about five personalities in every classroom: smart, not-so-smart, quiet, obnoxious, silly, (which is similar to, but not the same as) funny, and mean. Okay seven. And whether you have five students that fall into each of these personality types or just one, it still doesn't change the dynamic. And don't worry that you'll be missing one of the types. In the absence of one personality some enterprising student will fill the need.

I had stopped to share some gossip with Mr. Gloe, the third/fourth grade teacher, so by the time I entered the classroom; my students were already going about their routine. After all, it was December. They ought to know what they were about by then. They were coming and going, heading to their lockers, sharpening pencils, unloading books and hurrying to finish some forgotten homework.

Holly and David were standing at my desk, math books in hand, armed to the teeth with questions.

"Man, Mrs. Mudd," Holly drew out. "That coffee smells good."

"Back off!" I snapped, and then winked at Sophie who was smiling at me from her seat in the front row. Holly only managed a tired little giggle.

I patted my desk where I wanted Holly to set her book down and said to her, "Hold on," and then louder, even though—*God! When was my aspirin going to kick in*—my head was killing me.

"Okay. Your journal assignment is on the board. You need to get yourself together and start working. If, for some reason you've finished that—and I know you haven't since you haven't even started—you may read, or work on your book reports. But whatever you do, do it quietly, because I've got some people to talk...to...Patrick!" I spun around to face Patrick Gentry. *Whoa.* He was standing by the file cabinet looking through some papers.

Note to Self. Spinning: Bad.

"What are you doing?" I demanded.

"I'm looking for my math from yesterday."

"Can I ask why?"

"I had a question."

"Then why did you turn it in?"

"So I could be done and go to Art class like you said."

I, ever so slowly, turned my chair a quarter of the way back to level a look at Aaron, who was laughing quietly. After Aaron got back to work I turned back and called on all the patience I had to my name.

"Well, Patrick. Thank you for your honesty. But I will grade what you've turned in."

"What?!" He whined loudly, and I winced.

Yelling: Also bad.

"Go sit down."

He made a sound that, really, only a thirteen-year-old can make. "But, Mrs. Mudd, I didn't understand it..."

"Then you should have held onto it and asked me about it today." I waited a beat. "Like I *also* told you."

He looked at Holly and David, clearly in line to do just that. Then he gave me his version of The Look—which wasn't half bad—and returned to his desk to sulk.

I looked at Holly. "Alright girlie, what do you need?"

Later that morning, there was a funeral at the church. After the service, the family gathered for refreshments in the cafeteria. As it happened, there was a cooler full of lemonade left over that Rosemary placed on a table in the hallway.

She stopped by my classroom that afternoon and motioned for me to speak to her in the hall. "There's some leftover lemonade from the funeral," she said. "Have your kids finish it off, will you?"

"Well, sure. Thanks."

"Okay. I left cups right next to the cooler."

"Great. We're going outside this afternoon for a little while. They can drink it after that."

Shortly after, Greg asked to go to the restroom, and after him, Sophie, Jim and David. It had been a long afternoon so I didn't think anything of it. I was helping Carrie at her desk when I saw David re-enter the room and smile at Mike.

I didn't like that smile. That smile meant that something was going on that I was—at the moment—unaware of. I was instantly suspicious, so when Aaron asked to use the restroom I told him he could wait. He didn't seem overly disappointed, so that threw me off the scent.

"Is something wrong Mrs. Mudd?"

I tore my gaze from Mike to Carrie and smiled. She was always more sensitive to the moods of others.

"Nope. Not a thing." But then it hit me. They were drinking that lemonade. Those little bastards.

Outside that afternoon, I asked Aaron for his help with the cooler. Let me tell you a little bit about Aaron. He was the bee's knees to the girls in this school, and believe me when I say he knew it. But he was a nice kid when the mood was on him, and that's about all you can ask of a person his age.

"Man, this cooler feels like it's about half full."

I pretended to laugh. "Probably because Greg told all those guys to get a drink out of it when they went to the bathroom."

Aaron actually did laugh, completely unaware that he was about to fall for the oldest trick in the book. "Yeah...he tell you that?"

I shook my head. "No, but *you* just did."

And just before I started laughing, I had the pleasure if seeing him stop dead in his tracks, his expression blank with shock. Then he turned on me.

"Mrs. Mudd! Now why you gotta do that to me?" He looked over his shoulder. "Greg, I am so sorry, man... I think I just got you in trouble."

There are some who will suggest that during the exciting times of a school year a teacher needs to be tough on her kids. Put a little mean on. Lay down the law. Good luck with that, I always say. December is not the time to start drawing lines in the sand. Neither is May. Truly you have to be smarter than your students, not meaner than them. If it came down to a contest, you wouldn't be able to outdo a middle school student for sheer meanness. They're wily, and they're smart. I'll be honest; there were days that I struggled. Days that I was off my game and they got the best of me.

But then...there were also days that they didn't.

PART SIX:
ODDS AND ENDS

"I've never had a humble opinion.
If you've got an opinion, why be humble about it?"

~*Joan Baez, b. 1941*
American musician

From: Mona
Sent: Tuesday, February 21, 2006 7:34 AM
To: Cathy, Matt
Subject: EARLY this morning

At one o'clock in the morning I woke up to the sound of gagging that invariably precedes Maggie throwing up for the 5th time this weekend. So I was stripping sheets and doing laundry by 2:00…and, just for the heck of it, unloading the dishwasher by 2:15. It made me think of you and Matt, who say, "Somewhere, right now, there are people cooking dinner, giving baths, going to PTA meetings…" Now you can add another to your list, "Somewhere, right now, somebody is cleaning up puke…" It has a nice ring to it.

Reply All
From: Cathy

I can't believe you were up for that reason - and the fact you were unloading the dishwasher - what a shock!

Actually -I had an eventful morning myself....I had asked John to call me at 6:00 am my time, which is Central Standard Time… well- I guess he got a little confused b/c he called me at 4:00 am - needless to say, then I dozed in and out of sleep thinking about what I had to do today (fly to Chicago for meeting the rest of the week, go to the office before my flight, etc...) At least he called me back at 6:00 to be sure I was awake.

Bottom line - at least there was no puke involved!

Reply All
From: Matt

Oh puke sucks. We can also add somewhere someone right now is getting a speeding ticket.

Driving home from happy hour at about 10:30 PM tonight I have an officer pull me over. He said he was ticketing me for going 75 mph in a 60 mph zone. The whole thing took only about 10 minutes. The officer was very polite and even told me to pull out safely. Of course as I got back on the highway with my window safely rolled up I gave him my fantasy response: "Well, actually officer I'm a little drunk so if you can just leave your lights on until I'm back on the road I'd appreciate it. PS --I think your radar gun may be faulty -- I was actually going 82. I'm also really glad you've all stopped racial profiling. See you in court jackass 'cause I'm fighting this one!"

From: Matt
Sent: Tuesday, February 21, 2006 11:34 PM
To: Mona
Cc: Cathy
Subject: Here's another

Somewhere someone right now is having their Malaysian neighbor accost them at their doorstep at 11:00PM because he's obviously been waiting to hear your car door shut to ask you to pick up his UPS package (computer modem he claims) from his doorstep because he's driving to Columbia MO tomorrow.

Somewhere the kindly neighbor replies "Sure, what time is it being delivered?"

Somewhere the Malaysian terro... neighbor replies "Between

10AM-3PM."

Somewhere the kindly neighbor further asks "When will you be back from Columbia?"

Somewhere the Malaysian jihadi... I mean neighbor replies "5PM."

Somewhere the kindly neighbor responds "I won't be home until around 6PM."

Somewhere Osama-bin-Neighbor says "Well if it's here will you pick it up?"

Somewhere kindly homo neighbor replies "Not if it's ticking... but I will kick it behind your bushes." Okay, kindly homo neighbor really just replies "Yes."

Anyway I bet somewhere, somehow that really is happening to someone else too Now I know I just had a run in with the law and am a bit frazzled, but I still can't figure out why he would ask me to pick up his package if he's going to be home before me. Anyway, do they sell plutonium meter readers at Home Depot?

Chapter Twenty-One

Sometimes, when I'm out among strangers, I think it's entertaining to create a brand new life for myself. I don't do it out of malice, not on purpose anyway, and it's not something I do very often. But faced with someone I perceive to be gullible, I cannot resist its charm.

While at a restaurant, I'll tell the couple down the bar I'm in from Wisconsin, or moving to Nova Scotia in the fall. It no longer surprises my friends. In fact, they go along with it, mainly because there's not much else to do in Missouri but imagine a life elsewhere.

I once talked to a person for two hours who believed wholeheartedly I was in town from Manchester, Tennessee. Manchester is a small town off Highway 24, halfway between Chattanooga and Nashville, and I haven't seen it since I left twenty-six years ago, but my knowledge of its location lent a certain air of truth to my story that would have been absent otherwise.

I chose Tennessee because a slight southern accent is the only thing I feel comfortable imitating at length. I use too much of my mouth when I speak to pull off a clipped British accent, and I can't get the vowels right to be Australian.

So Tennessee it was, and I was a songwriter. I admitted to him, modestly, that I was pretty well known on Music Row. He was impressed that I co-wrote a song for Tracy Byrd, and as well he should have been. It's not exactly easy to write a song.

I spoke to Loretta Lynn one night at the Grand Old Opry, and had even met Reba McEntire once. They're both very nice, I told him, and not a single word of my story was true. It entertained me, though, which is more than I could say had he been left to his own devices, and it kept him from having to ask for my phone number.

"Long distance," he said, "it's a killer," and that was a blessing since I couldn't begin to produce a Tennessee area code.

But the worst lie I claim came one snowy night in winter, four weeks after giving birth to my daughter. Unfortunately, the beauty of childbirth didn't inspire my husband to do our Christmas shopping. So I found myself at the mall, wandering in and out of stores and trying to ignore the exhaustion rapidly taking hold.

Just before the mall closed for the evening, I headed to Sears. My mom had seen a vacuum cleaner she wanted, and in the months preceding Christmas had dropped enough hints that I understood I was supposed to give it to her.

I approached the counter and noticed the clerk, Sheila, beginning her closing routine. I assumed she could point me in the right direction. I'd buy the vacuum, and be on my way. I assumed too much, and soon found myself waiting for another employee to retrieve it from the warehouse in back of the store.

Sheila was obviously a person threatened by long silences, because she couldn't fill up the air fast enough while she rang me up and printed my receipt. I soon found that the price of a vacuum included an unholy amount of paperwork, and a set of impromptu verbal instructions from Sheila regarding the vacuum's assembly— which did me no good whatsoever because: One, I wasn't listening. And Two, the vacuum was nowhere in sight.

I had already bought the thing, giving Sheila no good reason to continue to sell it, but she had one at home and felt the need to rave about it as if she believed the vacuum to be smart rather than its manufacturer.

"The hose is constantly attached!" She raved. "It's not a separate attachment! You just lean over, clean that edge of carpet by the wall, then Bam! Put it back and it goes back to normal!"

She leaped from that topic straight into another, and my attention wandered in and out of her chatter. Sometime during her monologue it became clear to me why people commit homicide, even though I knew I wasn't being fair.

"...I have three," she was saying when I tuned in at one point, "a boy from my oldest and two girls from my only daughter..." and on she went, trotting out her family pictures, so I could confirm, on cue, that her grandchildren were beautiful.

Eventually my fatigue beat out any concern for social etiquette, and I sat down on the carpeted display between a cheap canister vacuum and a Bissell Upright. Sheila kept talking, and I began to wonder where they stocked the breast pumps since another problem had suddenly jumped ahead of the rest. Right then, Sheila took a moment to observe the proprieties and actually asked me about my own life. I told her I had two children, Will, who was nine years old, and Maggie, who was four weeks old.

"Ugh!" She exclaimed. "Why so far apart?"

My chin jerked up in surprise. *Why so far apart?* I admit that she caught me on a bad night, but her question struck me as rude. Like asking a couple why they don't have kids without any prior knowledge of their lifestyle, their personalities, or their fertility.

"Well, the youngest was a mistake." I announced.

Sheila seemed horrified by that. Whether she was affronted by the idea that anyone would have a child by mistake, or the fact that I would admit it, I'm not sure. It was a complete lie, of course, but the sudden urge to laugh felt good following the torture that had been the last twenty minutes. She schooled her expression, and in my imagination, I pictured what she would do with the truth—

"Well let's see, Sheila." I imagined saying. "I got pregnant at twenty with my son, but his dad left town. I had one failed marriage, but finally married a wonderful man. We suffered through one heartbreaking miscarriage..." and I could have gone on, but that scene didn't have enough comic value, or any for that matter, and all of the sudden I was in a comic sort of mood. So, instead...

"Whoops!" I barked and she flinched. "We're pregnant!"

I topped my announcement with a little laugh that, I felt, conveyed the perfect amount of desperate humor with just a touch of anger. I leaned on the counter with a heavy sigh and gnawed at my thumbnail.

Sheila took a deep breath and patted my arm. "Well...babies are the very best kinds of mistakes, don't you think?"

"I guess!" I spat out and dropped my hand on the counter with a thud. It was then I noticed the absence of my wedding ring— which made the icing on *that* cake absolutely delicious.

Sometimes I think about Sheila. I wonder if she still works at Sears. I never look for her when I'm there, and I admit I never will. Did she think about me after I left? Maybe said a prayer for me –or most likely my children— over her Christmas goose that year. And sometimes, when my conscience catches up me, I feel bad for my lie.

I wish she knew Will and I play a game of Parcheesi or Checkers nearly every evening before he goes off to bed. I wish she knew that Maggie and I dance every day to the country music on the kitchen radio. And while I'll never know if thoughts of me ever cross her mind, I wish she knew that I do love them both equally, but differently, and desperately.

From: Mona
Sent: Tuesday, January 25, 2004 7:48 PM
To: Girls, Matt, Mom
Subject: This week in Entertainment

1.The albinos are mad that one of the bad guys in "The DaVinci Code" is among their ranks. Dr. Reese complains, "The evil albino has become a Hollywood stock character." I want so much to say something snide about this, but he's right. I'm scared to death of albinos. I'd like to see them take it up with Dan Brown though, rather than Ron Howard.

2.Mariah Carey's new album is entitled The Something-Something of "Mimi," after a nickname given to her by her closest friends and family. I'm tempted to delve a little deeper there and see if these people are actually close to her, or if they are just pretending to be. With a nickname like Mimi, you can bet somebody's laughing at her behind her back. But I'm going for this one instead...

"Oh no. Is she changing her name?!" Some hardcore fans wondered. No. It's just something she "felt like expressing at the time."
I've got ten bucks for anybody who knows what that means.

3.King Kong will be hitting our theaters in December starring Cathy's favorite—Adrian Brody (wink, wink). Peter Jackson directed and he assures us they "went a little crazy with Kong doody." Seriously, how old is this guy?

Reply
From: Mom

Ramona,
1.Are you aware that Johnny Carson died? You haven't
mentioned it.
2.I got home tonight and there were six messages for me.
Among them is one from Lou: "Connie, I have to talk to you
about the shower. There is a big problem. Call me as soon as
possible." Should I be worried?
3.Like Mariah Carey, I also am going to change my name. So,
I remain,

Cici

Chapter Twenty-Two

On Valentine's Day of my twenty-second year I was involved in a car accident. I was sitting at an intersection waiting to turn left when I got my opportunity. I entered the intersection and began to make my left when ...Slam! Smacked by another driver in the rear of the driver's side. Launched into an uncontrollable spin, I finally came to an abrupt stop in the turning lane, facing the opposite direction, with the sound of my blinker and my windshield wipers very loud in the sudden and absolute silence.

I was completely disoriented. The car was totaled. For a moment, my mind was a complete blank, unable to form the thoughts telling me how this had come to pass. I had no idea how I had gotten into this situation and had no idea how to get out of it.

Blindsided, I think it's called.

And I don't think I'm exaggerating when I say that the feeling I had on that day was duplicated every afternoon I spent with my mom while she was going through menopause.

～

There are a great many people who use things like PMS, menopause, or alcohol to explain away behavior that is uncalled for or out of the ordinary. If you suspect that you are one of these people, knock it off. Don't excuse yourself with excuses. You make the rest of us look bad.

From what I've seen, these situations don't create certain behaviors out of the blue, as much as they simply enhance what is already there.

I, myself, am a bit of a bitch. I can hide it, or dress it up and take it out. But it's always there. Lurking. Two days a month I'm on a slow boil, and at the slightest provocation I strike. I snap at my kids. I yell at my husband. But what I don't do is lie to myself, or anyone else, and act like it's something new. It's no surprise to me. And do you know why? Because the other twenty-six days of my cycle I'm just as bitchy and snide and unforgiving...I'm just inclined to control it a little better.

I bring this all up to point out that my mom didn't suddenly develop any new characteristics during her menopausal experience, she just enlarged the existing ones.

For example, Mom's a heavy breather when she's mad. Upset her, and you'll get the Heavy Exhale from her. She did this so many times from May to September, I thought she permanently dropped her blood-oxygen levels.

Mom also has this desire to be well liked by everyone, in all walks of life. This is a little apple she picked up from my Grandma, and they are both equally successful at it. In and of itself, there is nothing wrong with the trait. Except, during menopause, she became a slave to it. She developed this twisted, driving need for everyone to see her as the best. Her single-minded pursuit to be the greatest person on the planet defied logic, common sense, and sometimes even personal safety.

Mom and I were shopping one day towards the end of my pregnancy with my daughter, Maggie. While there, Mom fell in love with a red "Baby's First Christmas" pajama set, and decided to buy it for Maggie.

As we were checking out, my husband's cousin, Jackie, walked in with her mother. Jackie, who had just given birth to her own daughter a few weeks before, had met my mom maybe once in her entire life. Possibly twice- but that's a long shot.

They had already seen us and were heading over, but Mom started waving at them anyway. She reminded me of a person signaling a long-lost relative in a crowded airport. It's me! She seemed to say. Over here!

As they were making their way over Mom whispered, "Tell me her name again."

"Jackie." I said.

"And the baby?"

"Peyton."

Before Mom even reached the cart she was beginning the strains of, "Oh your baby is so beautiful!" Which is fine, and it didn't surprise me as much as what she did next.

"Well, I got you a present!" She announced. Then rushed over to our cart, and pulled out the Christmas outfit.

But instead of pawning it off with any number of convenient excuses, like, "I got you something… I was going to send it to you… I'm so glad you're here…It'll save me the cost of shipping…" She looked at me and said, "Maggie just lost it! Ha! Ha! Ha! Ha! Ha!" Then, in a flurry of movement, she handed the outfit to Jackie, leaned over the baby and cooed, "She should have an outfit from her Aunt Connie. Yes she should!"

I swear to you. Never in my life had I seen such an impressive display of rampant gaiety.

Then Jackie, who I'm pretty sure didn't remember my mom's name until she just said it, is forced to be thankful for a gift that she knows was not originally intended for her. Worse, she has to do it in front of the person who the gift has just been stolen from. And just in case we didn't get it the first time, Mom started laughing again, darting her gaze back and forth to make sure everyone in the store was catching the true spirit of giving taking place by the exit.

"Ha! Ha! Ha! Ha!" She laughed. "It was for Maggie, and now it's for Peyton!"

She waved a dismissing hand at me. "Ramona, I hope you don't mind…"

I said, "Oh, no," and avoided making eye contact with Jackie who was looking at my mom and—probably not—thinking, *This woman is the nicest person on the planet.*

1.*I tuned in at about 7:11 and found that Keith Urban had already performed. Bummer. I was tempted to turn it off right then, but thank Christ I didn't, if only because now I know what he looks like when he gets out of bed.*

2. *Bridget called it. Two months ago she said Garth Brooks was slowly coming out of retirement- claimed they were playing his songs more on the radio. I told her she was crazy. My phone rang as soon as he took the stage. She didn't say hello, just. "Do you see that man standing on that stage?" I hung up on her.*

3.*Standing ovations seemed to be the order of the evening. I guess I always thought they were reserved for something really special. As it was- I could have walked onstage, done a cartwheel, and brought people to their feet*

4.*I hate, hate, hate it when people wear sunglasses indoors. Nothing says "pompous and self-absorbed" more clearly to me. Are the lights that bright? And if they are, then riddle me this: Why do the other 98% of artists not require protective eyewear?*

5.*Finally, and I cannot stress this enough. Appliqués- no matter how expensive- are not attractive.*

CHAPTER TWENTY-THREE

MY HUSBAND THINKS I'M TOO NOSY. He shakes his head. "You just love stuff that's none of your business..." he says.

And yes I do.

That's why I buy magazines that are filled from cover to cover with information that is, actually, none of my business. I practically fell apart from the lack of information regarding his mom's break up with her boyfriend two years ago. I gasped and said, "But, why?!"

He said, "I don't know. It was none of my business." Which sounded like a bunch of crazy talk to me. *I don't know? None of my business?*

Needless to say, I never did get the full story on that. By the time I got to her she was out of the emotional throes of the break up and into the "Oh well, water under the bridge" phase, and that's just not fun anymore.

I need emotion! I need high drama!

But, nosy as I am, rude as I am, there is a certain level that I do not and could not ever reach. That is to say that I will listen in on complete strangers, but I will never talk to them. I never ask questions or comment on the weather. I don't make small talk in line at the store, I don't give people directions at gas stations, and I don't offer advice to people who seem confused or indecisive. I hate it when people do it to me, and I try to return the favor one fine citizen at a time. Because, really, once you've spoken you have to keep on speaking.

Imagine you're standing in line at the grocery store and Mr. Phil Lichtakken says, "Hey. You look like you're having a get together." Let's ignore, for the moment, that he's staring at the contents of your cart which I think is creepy. So then you have to say something back. That, or pretend to be deaf, which, believe me, is a lot of work.

I would say something like, "Yep." And leave it at that. But people sense that about me and rarely offer conversation.

Instead Phil will find somebody who will say, "Yes. My husband is having a Super Bowl Party." Well, then, that pops the conversation wide open. Then they need to discuss who's going to win. Which player they like. Which player they sort of, kind of, know through a friend of a friend of a friend. And don't forget to tell them (a complete stranger who, believe me, does not care) where *you* are going to be on Super Bowl Sunday.

And God forbid there's a problem and the cashier has to turn on her blinking light, because then they have wait until the twenty-six-year-old balding Christian Republican manager comes jingling over and presses a few "special" keys that only he knows.

Then they'll get to watch him try to pass off a few words of friendly conversation to the cashier who he ignores most of the time because he's got an inflated view of himself that leads him to believe that she actually cares.

And so ALL THAT TIME they've got to continue this farce of a conversation about the freaking Super Bowl when neither one of them actually cares and only one of them is going to watch it.

From: Mona
Sent: Tuesday, June 07, 2005 8:00AM
To: Amy, Bridget
Subject: Sex and the City

Watched a rerun last night-the one where Charlotte and Harry got married. Best line:

"Last night Howie and I had sex like we were teenagers again. Meaning he didn't know what he was doing, and I didn't say anything."

I laughed so hard I almost fell off the couch.

Reply All
From: Bridget

… as Carrie has her head cocked to the side from all the jackrabbit sex and can't stand up straight. Oh, the horror.

Reply
From: Amy
To: Mona
Cc: Stagner, Bridget

Speaking of which…Guess who Stagner and I ran into at Busch Stadium last night?

Reply All
From: Mona

Dave Keaner

Reply All
From: Amy

Guess again. Note who is in the "to" line, vs. who is in the "cc."

Reply All
From: Mona

Oh! How is he?

Reply All
From: Amy

Good. Largest crowd at Busch since they took out a bunch of seats for the new scoreboard in 1997, and we run into old friends sitting two sections over and standing in the same beer line. Did you know Molly is due to have Baby #3 this week? I don't even think I knew she was pregnant again.

Reply All
From: Mona

Hmm. Jackrabbit indeed.

Chapter Twenty-Four

THERE ARE CERTAIN PEOPLE IN LIFE you can never really get away from, and the funny thing is you can't ever predict who these people are going to be. Suddenly, ten years after high school you find yourself working for someone you barely knew—who was a freshman when you were a senior. Twelve years after college, a classmate's daughter will be on the same soccer team as your daughter's. So, while you didn't have much in common twelve years ago, you find that now, sitting next to each other at all the games, you never run out of conversation. Life is a circle, spinning and overlapping itself, never giving away its secrets or its plan.

My friends tease me that the one person I will never really escape is my high school boyfriend Jack. We never see each other. But if we happen to, our stilted conversations make it quite apparent that we have nothing in common. So while I don't really know *him* anymore, I find that I still know everything *about* him.

I have a friend Angie who regales me regularly with stories of Jack and his wife, Molly. "Their kids are so cute!" She'll gush. "And so well behaved." And then I'll call Bridget and we'll discuss if I've done something wrong— no, scratch that—what specifically I did wrong to deserve this. I don't have anything against their kids. Lord, don't go accusing me of that. It's just that the hardest thing about the end of my high school years was watching Jack truly fall in love again with someone who was not me. Molly. Who is now his wife. Ouch.

I was forced to acknowledge in the end that she fit him in a way that I never could. She made him happy in a way that I never would. And while I suspect that relationship has been on the line a few times in its day, they managed to stick it out. Good for them. But I honestly don't need to hear about them and their unabashed bliss.

There's a big part of me that wishes them only happiness in their life together. But there's a smaller, meaner part of me that does not. I'm sorry, I don't. That doesn't mean I want him back, it just means I'm human. And nobody completely wishes the best for the one that got away. They may tell you that. They may tell themselves that. But it's a lie.

My son's school principal is Jack's aunt, so my girlfriends also tease me because I can't seem to escape his family, either. Will and his principal spend a lot of time together. So, lucky me, I spend a lot of time with her too. Once every couple of months, I walk in the school office to find Mrs. Kowalczak leaning on the door frame of her office and beckoning me with her index finger. And, feeling like I'm seventeen again, I mumble, "I'm coming," then drag my feet into her office. I shut the door behind me. Then dart a glance at my son, who's smiling at me from his favorite chair, and together we settle in for a lecture.

Here recently he and his friend Nathan have been accused of dropping pebbles down their pant legs while they act like they're dinosaurs taking a crap on the playground. Mrs. Kowalczak does her level best to act like this latest transgression is a felony. Will tries not to laugh, and I do too. Because, as Mrs. Kowalczak speaks, my imagination is already running away from me.

I wonder what would happen if I just stood up and left. Would she follow me out the door? Or would she sit there, shocked, with her half-finished sentence dangling in mid-air. I wonder...

What if I just glared at her, and responded with something unexpected?

"You wanna talk about inappropriate?" I imagine asking. "Let's talk about those shoes you're wearing..." Even though there's nothing wrong with her footwear. In fact, I can't even see it from where I sit. But I wonder what she would do if I said that.

Or worse, what if I turned absurdly hostile? What if I rose from my seat, eyes flashing, and shouted, "Oh yeah? Well, your nephew was supposed to take me to the Homecoming Dance and he didn't..." Then I'd fling myself back into the chair, real moody-like, and start sobbing right there in her office. Really, what would she do? What could she do if I decided to take our whole meeting in a new and totally unforeseen direction? Sure, I know I have the mentality of an eight-year-old, but it calms me. As if the only way I know how to behave like an adult is to act like a child in my head.

While there is a flippant side to me that finds my thoughts hysterically funny, there is also an introspective side, completely aware that I'm only marshalling my defenses. I feel protective of my son, and protective of myself, at times like that. For all of my bluster, I am easily reduced to that girl on the playground who nobody wanted to play with. That broken-hearted teenager who couldn't have what she wanted most. Or that young mother who had no idea what to do.

When any of those parts of me feel threatened, I close myself off. I will deal with the problem later, when it's not all coming at me at once. But at the moment, I'm just sitting in that office. I'm smiling at all the right times, and responding when I feel it's necessary. And honestly, I mean no disrespect. But I'm just pretending to listen. I'm just feigning concern.

I'm just faking normal.

From: Mona
Sent: Friday, January 14, 2005 9:17 AM
To: Girls
Subject: Me

Last night, Dan accused me of telling stories backwards, then expecting people to know what I'm talking about. Is there any truth to that?

Reply All
From: Amy

?what to truth any there is

Reply All
From: Mona

Very funny. Seriously, do I start at the end of a story then work my way back to the beginning? Apparently my stories are out of order and impossible to understand. I think it's all an elaborate excuse for why he doesn't think I'm funny.

Reply All
From: Lynn

You must be married to the wrong man. Kevin thinks you're a riot.

Reply All
From: Bridget

How do you tell a story backwards?

Reply All
From: Amy

Or, more specifically, how does someone with Mona's flair for the dramatic tell a story backwards? Mona- most of the time your stories seem to start at the verrrrry beginning, in an effort to set the tone, and draw as much of a reaction from your audience as has ever been achieved off-Broadway. I think his accusation is indicative of his lack of attention when the story begins. He just doesn't start listening until the end, and by then he doesn't know what you're talking about.

Reply All
From: Mona

Thank you all very much. Your responses will be stored in the vault with the rest of my ammunition, and brought out when I feel it's necessary.

THE END

KEY CONTRIBUTORS

DAN: Mona's husband. Works as an accountant. As a self-proclaimed "simple man," he finds Mona's range of emotion "exhausting" at times. Likes to hunt. Seldom indoors.

BRIDGET: Works in Sales. Wife, and mother of a son. Can never accurately quote anything—always misplaces or transposes words. Very classy. Rarely out of control. Laughs until she cries.

AMY: Works in public relations. Snappy dresser. Is known for saying things she hasn't thought of yet. Has the quickest wit of the entire group. Rarely out of control. Cries until she laughs.

STAGNER: First name also Bridget, but is known by last name to avoid confusion. Works in construction. Wife and mother of two boys. Funniest moment:

Stagner: "God, I can't wait until tomorrow."

Christian: "Why? What's tomorrow?"

Stagner: "Tomorrow I won't be hung over anymore."

CHRISTIAN: Wife, and mother to one son. Husband is gone all week, every week on business. Moved to Missouri from Maryland. Biggest complaint about her new hometown: People from Missouri constantly interrupt when you're tr—

MEGAN: Works with young children as a speech therapist. Kindergarten teacher-type. Nicest person on the planet. Tougher than you'd think. Best known for her sporadic, yet crushing, insults— all hilarious.

CATHY: Used to work with Bridget. Has been recently transferred to Arkansas for her job. Mona's frequent travel companion. Nicer than she lets on. Meaner than you can imagine. Funniest line (to some strangers annoyed by her cigarette smoking):
"Hey, guess what? It's not crack!"

MATT: Very, very funny. Works at a money lending company. Has begrudgingly been promoted to manager. Hates it. Cathy's best friend since middle school. Always quitting smoking.

LYNN: Wife, and mother of one daughter. Works as a respiratory therapist. Grew up three doors down from Mona and her best friend since the first grade. Often perceived as the sweetest, most kind-hearted member of the group. That perception is wrong.

MOM: Could be described in a million wonderful ways, but perhaps best known for her bits of advice which manage to be both completely useless, and amazingly helpful. When faced with one of life's struggles, she often says something like: "Well, Ramona. It's better than a poke in the eye with a sharp stick." Which is true enough, I suppose.

Printed in the United States
63863LVS00004BA/177